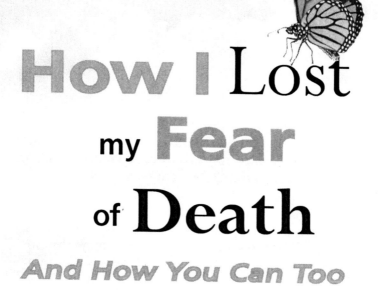

How I Lost my Fear of Death

And How You Can Too

Jack McElroy

How I Lost My Fear of Death
and How You Can Too

ISBN: 978-0-9860265-3-9
Library of Congress Control Number: 2013915264

All Scripture quotations, unless otherwise indicated, are taken from the King James Bible.

Interior design by Edie Glaser
www.craftingstones.com

McElroy Publishing
Transforming Hearts and Lives Since 1992

27-33 Fredonian Street
Shirley, MA 01464
978-425-4055
978-425-6116 (fax)
info@mcelroypublishing.com

DEDICATION

This book is dedicated to you, dear reader, for two reasons:

First, because you're courageously taking action to solve your fear of death problem. Many folks take the easy way out and either ignore their fear or just trust someone else's opinion without thinking for themselves.

Second, because you are a truth seeker. Truth seekers are a rare breed. Not many are willing to take the risk that what they've been taught or what they have believed in the past might be wrong.

But there's nothing like the feeling of peace you get when you know you've found the truth. I have this peace, and whether or not you agree with me, I encourage you to never quit searching until you have found it too.

Contents

The ultimate value of any religion is how well it relieves your fear of death. A religion must answer two questions if it is to be of any help: is there an afterlife, and if so, what must you DO to get there?

Compares Islam and Catholicism to show how most religions provide a "magic formula" for life after death.

Examines what Catholicism, Eastern Orthodoxy, Protestantism, Jehovah's Witnessism, and Mormonism teach about life after death.

Examines what Judaism, Islam, Hinduism, Sikhism, and Buddhism teach about life after death.

INTRODUCTION

T hey say you should never discuss religion or politics—but who really pays attention to that advice?

We all like to talk about religion because we like to compare our beliefs with each other.

And speaking of religion, the ultimate value of any religion is how well it does in relieving you of your fear of death.

Its ability to do that can be reduced to the answers it gives you to two questions:

1. What happens to you after you die? and assuming the answer is some promise of eternal life or something like it,

2. What do you have to *DO* to get the promise?

All religions promise something better in the hereafter. And they all prescribe rituals and works you have to *DO* to get it. The problem is that they never tell you when you've *DONE* enough.

1

Sometimes when you talk about religion, people get mad.

But that usually happens because someone tries to stuff their religion down your throat. You won't get that from me. I am a religious libertarian. I believe that you should be free to believe (or not) in any religion you want.

Here's what I mean . . .

You own your own life. No man has the right to own you. You have the liberty to choose your own belief system. To lose your liberty is to lose your life.

When you are afraid of death, you are controllable. All religions ultimately control you because they leave you in fear of death. They give you plenty to **DO** but never give assurance as to when you've **DONE** enough. You're constantly on the treadmill, and they make you afraid to get off.

All the chains that bind you are in your mind and imposed upon you by others. You don't need to let anyone be your master. You are free to choose for yourself. Don't let anybody take your liberty. To take life is murder, to take property is theft, but to take liberty is slavery.

You have the right to choose what and who you want to believe, and no one has the right to force or impose their religion upon you. You own your life and it is your right to choose who you will obey.

In this short book I'll make a case for my beliefs and how I came to them, but in the end you can decide for yourself if my conclusions are worthy of your consideration.

I hope the information in this book helps you to resolve your fear of death like it did for me.

Jack McElroy
August 2013

What Happens
After You Die?

Are you afraid to die?
I know how you feel. I used to be scared of dying too.

It's like being in bondage. No matter how hard you struggle, you can't get free. If you're like I was, then you're afraid to die because nobody ever gave you a good reason why you shouldn't be. That is, until now.

This report will set you free. It will give you the perfect reason why you won't need to be afraid to die anymore.

I feared death because of this nagging question...

What Happens after You Die?

In 1976, *Rolling Stone* named *(Don't Fear) The Reaper* by rock band Blue Öyster Cult the song of the year. And in 2004, it placed the song at number 397 on its list of "The 500 Greatest Songs of All Time."

The Reaper is about the inevitability of death and the foolishness of fearing it. The lyrics say "Romeo and Juliet are together in eternity," leading you to believe there is a continuation of life after death. The song continues . . .

We can be like they are.

And the refrain goes like this:

Come on baby (Don't fear the reaper)
Baby take my hand (Don't fear the reaper)
We'll be able to fly (Don't fear the reaper)
Baby I'm your man.

Some people, like the members of this band, believe in an afterlife that's attainable for everyone. Which is pretty cool—if true. You get "in" automatically when your body dies. This is basically what you were taught if you were brought up as a Christian Scientist or Unitarian.

It's also the view of folks who have a "religious" background but no longer practice their religion. Believing this makes you feel better for a time, but the problem is that this belief is subjective. These people can't take away your fear of dying, because there is no foundation under their belief other than their own opinion.

Others believe that when you're dead, you're dead—The End. Atheists and many others believe this. Their view is that all religions are the result of ignorance or superstition. I half believed this for a while too. For me, it is the most negative, depressing, and hopeless belief system out there.

But you know what? I knew in my heart it wasn't true. Common sense and deductive reasoning told me there is a God.

Deductive reasoning is "big picture." It's also known as "top down" logic. You start out with a generalization and follow a process to reach a specific, logical conclusion.

There has to be a God. All of creation and the orderly, integrated systems that synergistically exist scream it. I denied God because, quite honestly, I didn't want to be accountable to him.

Interestingly, there is an atheist site that says:

The death of a loved one can be heart-breaking. Contemplating our own deaths can produce anxiety. So it is perfectly understandable that many wish that they and those close to them could somehow survive their deaths. Wishes are not the best guides for life, however.[1]

Atheist Bus Campaign creator Ariane Sherine and Richard Dawkins at its launch in London.

The writer says "Contemplating our own deaths can produce anxiety." No kidding. That's the point. Despite their assurances that life after death is a vain hope, atheists can't prove their position either. I guess they'll find out for sure someday.

Most people believe that there has to be something more. You probably do too. Every religion in the world believes that there is.

Whether you were brought up Catholic, Protestant, Eastern Orthodox, Jehovah's Witness, Mormon, Jewish, Muslim, Buddhist, or in pretty much any other religion, you should know they all agree on one key point.

Without exception, these religions agree that it is necessary for you to DO certain "good works" in order to obtain life after death (or nirvana/peace).

THE MAGIC FORMULA FOR LIFE AFTER DEATH

The magic formula basic to all these religions is a combination of three things:

1. Have faith in God (or gods if you are a Hindu).

2. Keep certain laws.

3. Observe certain religious rituals.

For example, if you are Muslim, you must observe the . . .

Five Pillars of Wisdom

1. **Make a confession of faith** (*the shahada*) by declaring, "There is only one God and that God is Allah and Mohammed is His prophet." (By the way, Allah is a God who does not have a son. More on that later.)

2. **Pray** five times a day (*salat*).

3. **Give alms** to the poor (*zakat*).

4. **Fast** during the month of Ramadan (*sawm*).

5. **Make a pilgrimage to Mecca** (the Hajj).[2]

If you are Roman Catholic, you must observe the . . .

Seven Sacraments

In addition to believing in God and his son (whose name is Jesus Christ) and keeping the commandments of God and the Church, you must also observe certain rituals known as sacraments:[3]

1. Baptism

2. Penance or Reconciliation

3. Eucharist

4. Confirmation

5. Matrimony

6. Holy Orders (by which a man is made a bishop, a priest, or a deacon)

7. Anointing of the Sick (or Extreme Unction)

Here's what it looked like in the old *Baltimore Catechism* of the Roman Catholic Church:[4]

The Seven Sacraments Instituted by Christ to give grace.

These seven "Power Houses" make this the safest road to heaven.

In the end, all religions mostly tell you that if you don't have faith, keep the law, and do the religious rituals that they prescribe, then there's going to be . . . "hell to pay," or something like it.

Speaking of religions, let's take a closer look at what some religions say about an afterlife . . .

Is There an **Afterlife?**

What the Religions Say

Almost all religions say there is some kind of afterlife. Although there are some exceptions:

⇨ **Humanism** lays no claim to any God, and the second Humanist Manifesto states: "There is no credible evidence that life survives the death of the body. We continue to exist in our progeny and in the way that our lives have influenced others in our culture." Interestingly, they go on to say . . . "No deity will save us; we must save ourselves."[1]

It's also fascinating that John Dewey (1859–1952), known as the *Father of American Education,*

13

was one of the original signers of the first *Humanist Manifesto* in 1933. Unlike the later ones (there are now three), the first *Manifesto* talked of a new "religion," and referred to Humanism as a religious movement to transcend and replace previous religions.[2]

If you ever wondered whether there is a "state" religion in the United States, humanism is it. But that's a discussion for another time.

Do all roads lead to the same afterlife?

✍ **Confucianism** has no deities and no teachings about the afterlife.

✍ **Taoism** recognizes lots of gods and goddesses and also focuses on this life rather than an afterlife.

✍ **Shintoism** ("Way of the Gods") is the religious persuasion of many Japanese people. There is no doctrine in Shinto regarding the nature of life after death. Shinto is wholly devoted to life in this world and emphasizes man's essential goodness.[3]

There is an old saying in Japan: "born Shinto, die Buddhist." We'll take a closer look at Buddhism later.

These four religions don't focus on life after death but instead teach morality for the here-and-now.

What's interesting is that Humanism, Confucianism, Taoism, and Shintoism, which downplay (or deny) any afterlife, still instruct you to do certain "good works." And what do you get for a reward beyond the grave? Nothing. You just end up dead.

Now that really stinks.

The rest of the major religions have rules and regulations to tell you how to obtain eternal life. So why don't we lay them out on the table and see if we can find a pattern and dispel the fear.

But before we get started, let me give you a little bit of my background.

I was brought up Roman Catholic.

I attended Rose Hawthorne Central Catholic School in Concord, Massachusetts, where nuns taught me from pre-primary through eighth grade. I was taught by Jesuits at St. Francis Xavier High School, also in Concord. I received all of the sacraments, except Extreme Unction and Holy Orders, and was married at Sacred Heart Parish in Groton, Massachusetts.

As a young person, I tried to keep the commandments and live in a state of grace. I hoped that when I died I would be "good enough" to at least make it to purgatory. As I got older, I found it more and more difficult to keep the commandments and finally just quit trying. By the time I graduated from college, I didn't much believe in anything.

I'll share more on this later, as well as exactly how I lost my fear of death, but first, let's look at what the religions say you must DO to live forever.

One thing I want you to understand is that almost all religions have in common this teaching—that eternal life is . . .

A "Do-It-Yourself" Program

DO this, **DO** that, pray these prayers, keep certain days holy, receive certain sacraments, be a good person, be baptized, confess your sins, do unto others, offer up your sufferings, et cetera.

It doesn't matter which religion you pick, they all have a list:

- ✓ Catholicism has its DOs.
- ✓ Protestantism has its DOs.
- ✓ Eastern Orthodoxy has its DOs.
- ✓ Jehovah's Witnessism has its DOs.
- ✓ Mormonism has its DOs.
- ✓ Judaism has its DOs.
- ✓ Islam has its DOs.
- ✓ Hinduism has its DOs.
- ✓ Buddhism has its DOs.

They all tell you what you have to DO (or must not do) in order to qualify for life after death.

What's ironic is that **not one of them** will ever tell you . . .

when you've DONE enough.

If your religion names the name of Christ (which includes Mormonism, Jehovah's Witnessism, Eastern Orthodoxy, Protestantism, and Roman Catholicism), then you've probably been taught that "getting to heaven," or getting life after death, requires a combination of (1) faith in Jesus, and (2) your "good works." Those works would include keeping the commandments of God and the particular church or organization.

But have you ever been told what the deal is? What percent is Christ's work and what percent is yours?

What If You're Roman Catholic?

Roman Catholicism is one of the largest religions on earth claiming over one billion members.[4] If you weren't brought up Catholic, you could convert through the Rite of Christian Initiation of Adults. Film stars John Wayne, Gary Cooper, Faye Dunaway, Susan Hayward, and comedian Bob Hope are some of the more famous converts.[5]

Since I was brought up Catholic, let's start with what **Catholicism** says about how to obtain eternal life.

St. Peter's Basilica in Rome

According to the official *Catechism of the Catholic Church* (CCC), you "attain" salvation through (1) faith, (2) baptism, and (3) observing the commandments.

The Council of Trent (1545–1563) teaches that the Ten Commandments are obligatory for Christians and that the justified man is still bound to keep them; the Second Vatican Council (1962–1965) confirms: "The bishops, successors of the apostles, receive from the Lord . . . the mission of teaching all peoples, and of preaching the Gospel to every creature, so that all men may attain salvation through faith, Baptism and the observance of the Commandments" (CCC 2068).[6]

The Council of Trent codified longstanding church dogma. So despite what most Catholics think today, nothing about **you earning** eternal life by faith **plus** your own effort has changed in the Catholic Church in the past 400+ years.

Take a look at this little card I found a number of years ago teaching you how to save your own soul.

St. James Church
WEST GROTON, MASS.
REV. OSCAR R. O'GORMAN, Pastor
NOV. 2nd to NOV. 9th, 1941.

SAVE YOUR SOUL!

1. Receive regularly the Sacraments of Penance and the Holy Eucharist.
2. Say your morning and evening prayers. Make acts of Faith, Hope and Charity every day; at night, before retiring, examine your Conscience and make an act of Contrition.
3. Attend Mass on all Sundays and Holy Days of Obligation.
4. If there exist any Church Societies in your parish, join at least one of them.
5. It is an obligation to contribute to the support of the Church, binding under sin.
6. You are obliged to avoid the Occasions of Sin; an occasion of sin is any person, place or thing which will likely lead you into sin.
7. Practice Daily Devotion to the Blessed Virgin: pray to her particularly for the grace of a Happy Death.
8. Remember: Death — Judgment — Heaven — Hell, and you will persevere to end.

hew F. Sheehan Co., 22 Chauncy Street, Boston

The nuns taught me that I had to receive the sacraments, keep the commandments of God and the Church, and die in a state of grace to make it to heaven.

If you or I died with venial (small) sins on our souls, then we'd have to suffer in purgatory for an unspecified amount of time to pay the price for our own sin. Kind of makes sense, because everybody knows there's a price to pay for sin.

The whole idea of purgatory actually fits in with the works that we need to DO, because we'd be redeeming ourselves after death by suffering. Strangely, it turns out that purgatory is not even in the Bible. That was a shocker for me. Check it out for yourself.

Get a concordance; look up the word "purgatory." You won't find the word mentioned even once. There are about 790,000 words in the Bible, and not one is about you paying the price for your own sins in some place called purgatory.

Surprising, isn't it?

Oddly enough, even though purgatory doesn't appear in one Bible verse, the Catholic Church still teaches it. Masses and works continue to be offered for the souls who are supposedly there.

Now, the Church teaches that Jesus died on the cross "for our sins." Which is a great thought.

I mean, wouldn't it be great if somebody else paid for our sins instead of us?

But here's the thing, if there was such a place as purgatory, then you could pay the price for your own sins. If you could DO it, then all that Jesus DID was not enough to save you. You'd still have to earn it on your own—the hard way. So Jesus' death kind of doesn't do you much good.

And by the way, contrary to what most Catholics believe today, the Church still teaches that if you die with a mortal sin on your soul, you'll go straight to hell. That's right. Like purgatory, the whole idea of hell never went away, either.

Let me prove it to you.

Here's what the **New** *Catholic Catechism* says:

> Mortal sin . . . results in the loss of charity and the privation of sanctifying grace, that is, of the state of grace. If it is not redeemed by repentance and God's forgiveness, it causes **exclusion from Christ's kingdom.**[7]

"Exclusion from Christ's kingdom" is the politically correct way of saying you go to hell. But that's not the way it used to be. They weren't afraid to mention hell back in the old days, as you can see on the "Save your Soul" card from 1941. Notice the eight things mentioned that you must **DO** to "save your soul" on page 20. They are just the tip of the iceberg.

Here's what you are instructed to DO:

1. Receive the sacraments.

2. Pray and do good works.

3. Avoid sin.

Speaking of sin, it might be helpful to look at what the Church defines as "mortal." The kind that can send you to hell.

What Kind of Sins Are Mortal?

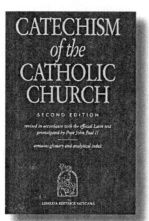

The nuns taught us that for a sin to be mortal:

1. It has to be a **"grave"** matter.

2. We must know it is wrong.

3. We must fully consent to it.

Here's a list of **"grave"** matters from the official *Catechism of the Catholic Church* (CCC).[8] I'm including this sort of lengthy list because it is

"10 Commandments" based—which Judaism, Catholicism, Orthodoxy, and Protestantism hold out as moral standards.

Violating the **First** Commandment:

📖 YOU SHALL WORSHIP THE LORD YOUR GOD AND HIM ONLY SHALL YOU SERVE.

× **Idolatry**—Worship, veneration, or belief in false gods is a **grave** sin.

× **Divination, magic, and sorcery**—These **grave** sins include attempting to command the powers of the occult, control or speak to demons or spirits (especially Satan), attempting to divine the future, and the use of magic charms (CCC 2116).

× **Sacrilege**—This **grave** sin consists of profaning or treating unworthily the sacraments and liturgical actions of the Church as well as things consecrated to God (CCC 2120).

× **Atheism**—Because atheistic humanism falsely seeks man and human glory and rejects God, atheism is a **grave** sin (CCC 2125).

Violating the **Second** Commandment:

📖 YOU SHALL NOT TAKE THE NAME OF THE LORD YOUR GOD IN VAIN.

✕ **Blasphemy**—This **grave** sin is the uttering of hatred, reproach, defiance, or speaking ill of God. Blasphemy against the Church, the saints, and sacred things is also a **grave** sin (CCC 2148).

✕ **Perjury and False Oaths**—Those who take an oath in the name of the Lord and fail to keep it, or break the oath at a later date, show a **grave** lack of respect for the Lord of all speech (CCC 2152).

Violating the **Third** Commandment:

📖 REMEMBER THE SABBATH DAY, TO KEEP IT HOLY.

MORTAL SIN

✕ **Deliberate failure of the Sunday obligation**—All Christians are bound to participate in the Mass and must partake of the Eucharist at least on holy days of obligation. Deliberate failure to do this constitutes a **grave** sin (CCC 2181).

Violating the **Fifth** Commandment:

📖 You shall not kill.

✕ **Murder (intentional homicide)**—Direct and intentional killing is **grave**ly sinful (CCC 2268).

✕ **Abortion**—All Catholics who procure a completed abortion or participate in execution of an abortion are automatically excommunicated from the Catholic Church (CCC 2272, CIC Canon 1314).

✕ **Euthanasia**—The direct killing of the sick, handicapped, or dying, regardless of motive, is a **grave** sin. The will and action taken to cause a person's death is an act of murder (CCC 2277).

× **Suicide**—Suicide is murder of the self. It is contrary to the love of God, self, family, friends, and neighbors (CCC 2281).

× **Scandal**—This is an attitude or behavior that leads another to do evil. If someone is deliberately led into a **grave** offense, that person's tempter commits a **grave** sin (CCC 2284, 2285).

× **Drug abuse**—Such abuse does **grave** damage to health and life and is a **grave** offense. Only legitimate therapeutic use is acceptable (CCC 2290).

× **Gluttony**—An excessive love for food and a disordered passion for worldly appetites is contrary to the virtue of temperance; it can constitute a **grave** sin. Gluttony is also a capital sin (CCC 1866, 2290).

× **Alcohol Abuse**—This type of abuse can also be excessively dangerous and harmful to the body, and sometimes to neighbors (CCC 2290).

MORTAL SIN

✕ **Terrorism**—Anything that threatens, wounds, and kills indiscriminately is of **grave** matter (CCC 2297).

✕ **Extreme Anger**—Anger is a desire for revenge. If anger reaches the point of a deliberate desire to kill or seriously wound a neighbor, it is **grave**ly against charity; it is a mortal sin (CCC 2302).

✕ **Hatred**—To deliberately wish a neighbor evil is a **grave** sin (CCC 2303).

✕ **Extortion**—To obtain something from another by coercion or intimidation is an act of violence and theft and is condemned by 1 Corinthians 6:9–10.

Violating the **Sixth** Commandment:

📖 You shall not commit adultery.

✕ **Adultery**—A married person who has sexual relations with anyone but their lawful spouse, even transient sexual relations, commits adultery (CCC 2380).

✕ **Divorce**—The **grave** sin of divorce condemns those who divorce and remarry

(Matthew 5:32) and those who divorce in the civil sense (except by **grave** dispensation). Hence, divorce between two baptized Christians is a mortal sin (CCC 2384).

× **Fornication**—The carnal union between an unmarried man and an unmarried woman is a **grave** sin (CCC 2353).

× **Pornography**—The display of intimate real or simulated sexual acts to a third party perverts sex and removes the marriage act from within the sacramental sanctity of marriage; it is **grave**ly contrary to charity (CCC 2354).

× **Prostitution**—Reducing a person to an instrument of sexual pleasure and lust is **grave**ly contrary to charity and chastity and defiles the body, the temple of the Holy Spirit. However, destitution, blackmail, or social pressure can reduce the gravity of the sin. Still, prostitution is *always* a sin (CCC 2355).

MORTAL SIN

× **Rape**—A person who commits rape violates the respect, freedom, and physical and moral integrity of the victim. It is a brutal crime of violence that can physically and psychologically scar a person for life. It is thus a **grave** sin (CCC 2356).

× **Homosexual acts**—Although it remains to be determined if homosexuality is a genetic, social, or personal stigma, homosexual acts are condemned by God and can NEVER be approved by the Church (1 Corinthians 6:9–10, Genesis 19:1–29, Romans 1:24–27, and CCC 2357). If homosexuals are born with the condition, then they are called to live a life of Christian purity and chastity for the greater love of Christ. Such people can experience a life of trial, which all others must treat with compassion and sensitivity.

× **Incest**—"Incest is intimate relations between relatives or in-laws within a degree that prohibits marriage between them" (CCC 2388).

× **Masturbation**—"Masturbation is the deliberate stimulation of the sexual organs in order to derive sexual pleasure" (CCC 2352). Masturbation violates both aspects of the natural law and is thus a **grave** sin.

Violating the **Seventh** Commandment:

📖 YOU SHALL NOT STEAL.

× **Theft**—All persons have a right to lawful private property obtained by legitimate work, inheritance, or gift. To violate a person's right to property by theft is a **grave** sin, especially if the loss of the property will severely hurt the victim (CCC 2408). The gravity of theft is determined by the harm it does to the victim. A poor beggar who steals a loaf of bread commits a less **grave** sin than a rich man who steals the savings of a destitute person. St. Paul tells us that thieves shall not inherit the kingdom of God (1 Corinthians 6:9–10).

MORTAL SIN

✕ **Cheating**—A cheater defrauds his victim of their property. It is morally of **grave** matter unless the damage to the victim is unusually light (CCC 2413).

✕ **Defrauding a worker of his wages**—This is one of the sins that cry to heaven for vengeance. Defrauding a worker of his wages withholds and impedes his ability to sustain basic needs for himself and his family (CCC 1867).

✕ **Unfair wagers**—Unfair wagers in games of chance are of **grave** matter if they deprive someone of what is necessary to provide for his needs and those of others (CCC 2413).

✕ **Taking advantage of the poor**—The economic or social exploitation of the poor for profit harms the dignity and natural rights of the victim. It is also a sin that cries to heaven for vengeance (CCC 1867).

Violating the **Eighth** Commandment:

📖 **You shall not bear false witness against your neighbors.**

✕ **False witness and perjury**—False witness is a public statement in court contrary to the truth. Perjury is false witness under oath. Both acts are **grave**ly sinful when they condemn the innocent, exonerate the guilty, or increase punishment of the accused. They are of **grave** matter because they contradict justice (CCC 2476).

✕ **Adulation**—Verbal speech or an attitude that encourages or confirms another in malicious acts and perverse conduct is a **grave** sin if it makes one an accomplice in another's vices or **grave** sins (CCC 2480).

✕ **Lying**—The most direct offense against the truth, lying is **grave**ly sinful when it significantly degrades the truth. The gravity of this sin is measured by the truth it perverts,

MORTAL SIN

the circumstances, intentions of the liar, and harm done to the victims (CCC 2484). Lying is a sin that originates from the devil, Satan, who is "the father of all lies" (John 8:44).

Violating the **Ninth** Commandment:

📖 YOU SHALL NOT COVET . . . YOUR NEIGH-BOR'S WIFE.

✗ **Lust** — A disordered desire for or inordinate enjoyment of sexual pleasure, lust is disordered because sexual pleasure must not be isolated from its true, natural place: within the Sacrament of Matrimony that is ordered to procreation of children and a unifying love between husband and wife (CCC 2351).

Violating the **Tenth** Commandment:

📖 YOU SHALL NOT COVET . . . ANYTHING THAT IS YOUR NEIGHBOR'S.

× **Avarice**—Greed and the desire to amass earthly goods without limit displays itself as a passion for riches and luxury. Those who seek temporal happiness at the expense of spiritual duties risk the **grave** sin of avarice. Avarice is one of the deadly vices (CCC 2536).

× **Envy**—This is another capital sin; it is sadness at the sight of another's goods and the immoderate desire to acquire them for oneself. Envy can lead to **grave** consequences and can harm neighbors. If envy leads to **grave** harm to a neighbor, it is surely a **grave** sin.

Probably no one will argue too much with this list of what constitutes "sin." We all easily recognize sin when somebody does it—especially if they sin against us. Anyway, it's the next section that gets a little dicey.

We're not DONE yet,
there's more . . .

MORTAL
SIN

Offenses Against Faith:

✕ **Voluntary doubt of faith**—Disregarding the revealed truth of God and his Church puts you at risk of spiritual blindness and loss of faith (CCC 2088).

✕ **Incredulity, heresy, apostasy, schism**—Incredulity is the neglect of revealed truth or willful refusal to assent to it. Heresy is obstinate post-baptismal denial of a truth that must be believed with divine and catholic faith. Apostasy is total repudiation of the Christian faith. Schism is the refusal of submission to the Roman Pontiff or communion with the members of the Church (CCC 2089). These sins strain or break the bonds of unity with the offender and the Catholic Church.

Offenses Against Hope:

✕ **Despair in hope**—Those who despair in hope cease to hope in salvation from God or help in attaining forgiveness of sin (CCC 2090). Christian hope sustains a believer's faith and dependence on God, and should not be neglected or rejected.

× **Presumption**—The Church teaches two types of sinful presumption: the presumption that man can save himself without help from God and the presumption that God's power or his mercy will merit a man forgiveness without repentance and conversion (CCC 2092).

Offenses Against Charity:

× **Indifference**—This **grave** sin entails neglect or refusal of divine charity (a.k.a. divine love). Those who sin in indifference fail to consider the goodness of charity and deny its power (CCC 2094).

× **Ingratitude**—An ungrateful sinner fails or refuses to acknowledge and return the love and charity of God (CCC 2094).

× **Lukewarmness**—Negligence in response to God's charity; it can also mean the refusal to

OFFENSES
AGAINST
FAITH
HOPE
CHARITY

give oneself to the prompting of charity (CCC 2094).

× **Acedia (spiritual sloth)**—This **capital** sin is the refusal of joy that comes from God. A sinner who indulges in acedia may even be repelled by divine goodness (CCC 2094).

× **Hatred of God**—This **grave** sin is born of pride and is contrary to the love of God. A sinner who hates God willfully rejects him. Hatred of God refuses to acknowledge and praise God's goodness and rejects obedience to him (CCC 2094).

As you can see, there's quite a list of DONTs—especially if you live in the real world.

Everybody I hung out with as a teenager broke some of these commandments. And it didn't get better in college and beyond. No wonder kids quit going to church. Plus, that list doesn't even include small (venial) sins.

And how about "indifference," "ingratitude," and "spiritual sloth"? Who knew?

Oh, and did you notice the **"Deliberate failure of the Sunday obligation"** commandment? That means you have to go to Mass once a week or it's a mortal sin. Many Catholics today don't go to Mass and pass it off as if it's not required.

But as you've seen, it still is. Nothing has changed. The Church still teaches that deliberately missing Mass on Sunday or a holy day of obligation can wind you up in hell if you die with that sin on your soul.

With all this commandment burden, how are you supposed to lose your fear of dying?

What if you die suddenly with one or more of these sins laid to your account? What if you didn't do enough to earn eternal life? What if you end up lost forever? How can you have any peace of mind if you die and discover you left something out?

It's too bad the "Jesus" presented by the Church couldn't have done more to help Catholics make it. It's no wonder that many older Catholics turn instead to the Blessed Mother for help (just like it says on the "Save Your Soul" card on page 20).

What If You're Eastern Orthodox?

The Eastern Orthodox Church (including Greek and Russian Orthodox) is the second largest Christian Church in the world with an estimated 225–300 million members.[9]

Famous converts to this religion include film star Tom Hanks and, reportedly, New York Yankee Alex Rodriguez.[10]

If you grew up in this religion, you know that Orthodox Church beliefs regarding the attainment of eternal life includes a faith plus good works program. Not surprisingly (because of their common history) it closely mirrors the faith plus good works dogma of Roman Catholicism.

What If You're Protestant?

Many Protestant churches don't require observance of sacraments but do teach that your "good deeds" must outweigh your "bad deeds." Nice thought. But how would you ever know if they did? Are you supposed to wait till you die and hope for the best? How is that supposed to give you peace?

But let's move on to some other "Christian" religions . . .

What If You're a Jehovah's Witness?

The Jacksons (Michael, Janet, La Toya, and their siblings), tennis stars Venus and Serena Williams, and supermodel Naomi Campbell are some of the more well-known Witnesses.[11] The Jacksons are now lapsed members.

Why they keep knocking at your door . . .

If you were brought up as a Jehovah's Witness, then you know that you are commanded to go out and witness for Jehovah and his organization.

You were taught that the Jehovah's Witnesses . . .

> are united by common goals. Above all, we want to honor Jehovah, the God of

the Bible and the Creator of all things.
We do our best to imitate Jesus Christ
and are proud to be called Christians.[12]

The Governing Body of the Jehovah's Witnesses
in Brooklyn, New York, claims that Witnessism is
the only true religion. Funny, I was taught the exact same thing about being a Roman Catholic. We
were "The One True Church." Be that as it may . . .

> **The Jehovah's Witnesses** teach that sal-
> vation is possible only through Christ's
> ransom sacrifice and that individuals
> cannot be saved until they repent of their
> sins and call on the name of Jehovah.
> Salvation is described as a free gift from
> God, but is said to be unattainable with-
> out good works that are prompted by
> faith. The works prove faith is genuine.[13]

It's clear. Salvation is through (1) Christ's ransom sacrifice, (2) repentance of your sins, (3) call-
ing on the name of Jehovah, and (4) doing "good
works."

There had to be a do-it-yourself component.
And as you can see, there is.

Notice that salvation is called a "free gift," BUT
you can't get the gift without purchasing it with
your good works. So it's not exactly free, is it?

Jehovah's Witnesses go door to door to prove their faith.

For example, you are expected to spend a certain number of hours per week in door-to-door visitation, witnessing, giving away *Awake* magazine, selling subscriptions to *The Watchtower* magazine, and conducting Bible studies in the homes of converts.

> Preaching is said to be one of the works necessary for salvation, both of themselves and those to whom they preach. They believe that people can be "saved" by identifying God's organization and serving God as a part of it.[14]

Your ultimate goal is to prove yourself faithful to Jehovah, and if you are found faithful, you will be resurrected from the dead. In short, you must:

- ✓ "Come to Jehovah's organization" for salvation, and then

- ✓ Comply with the teachings.[15]

But what's the definition of "faithful"? How do you know that you're in a state of faithfulness when you die? What happens if you have a bad day and your "faithfulness" isn't up to par?

It's another do-it-yourself operation. You have a list of DOs and DONTs, but you're never sure when you've DONE enough. How are you supposed to lose your fear of dying if you're not sure when you've DONE enough?

If you don't come to Jehovah's organization, you won't end up in hell, but you will get annihilated. You will cease to exist.

You know what? Unfortunately, the "Jesus" presented by the Jehovah's Witnesses just didn't DO enough to help Jehovah's Witnesses obtain eternal life. We'll see more about this later on, first . . .

Mormon Temple
in Salt Lake City, Utah

What If You're Mormon?

There are lots of famous **Mormons** like the Osmonds, former 49ers quarterback Steve Young, U.S. Republican presidential candidate Mitt

Romney, and actress Katherine Heigl (*Under Siege 2: Dark Territory, 27 Dresses,* and other films).[16]

And they're very nice people too.

If you were brought up in this faith, you are required to combine faith and good works in order to gain eternal life.

Did Donnie and Marie teach you any of the following?

"We believe that through the Atonement of **Christ**, all mankind may be saved, by **obedience to the laws** and ordinances of the Gospel" (Articles 3 of the Articles of Faith). Now, that you may understand the meaning of this statement I cite some words written in one official Mormon publication titled *What The Mormons Think of Christ* by B. R. McConkie: " . . . All men, by the grace of God, have **the power to gain eternal life. This is called salvation by grace coupled with obedience to the laws and ordinances of the gospel.**"[17]

Notice that you have the "power to gain" eternal life. You have to DO it.

The Mormons teach that you must be baptized in water, completely and permanently repent of all sin, and **DO** many other good works in order to be saved.

Here's what is expected . . . [18]

✓ The Book of Mormon says of salvation: "for we know that it is by grace that we are saved, **after all that we can do**" (*Book of Mormon*, 2 Nephi 25:23).

✓ The LDS [Latter Day Saints] Third Article of Faith states: "We believe that through the Atonement of Christ, all mankind may be saved, **by obedience to the laws and ordinances of the gospel**" (*Pearl of Great Price: Articles of Faith*).

✓ Joseph Fielding Smith explains what that last phrase means: "that which **man merits through his own acts** through life and **by obedience to the laws and ordinances** of the gospel" (*Doctrines of Salvation*, vol. 1, p. 134).

✓ James Talmage explains: ". . . redemption from personal sins can only be obtained through **obedience** to the requirement of **the Gospel, and a life** of good works" (James Talmage, in *A Study of the Articles of Faith*).

✓ Spencer W. Kimball states: "however powerful the **saving grace of Christ, it brings exaltation to no man who does not comply with the works of the gospel**" (*The Miracle of Forgiveness*, p. 207); "Each command we obey **sends us another rung up the ladder** to perfected manhood and toward godhood; and every law disobeyed is a sliding toward the bottom where man merges into the brute world" (*Teachings of Spencer W. Kimball*, p. 153); "living **all** the commandments **guarantees total forgiveness of sins** and assures one of exaltation . . . **trying is not sufficient. Nor is repentance** when one merely tries to abandon sin" (*The Miracle of Forgiveness*, pp. 164–165, 354–355).

✓ Bruce McConkie claimed: "Jesus kept the commandments of his Father and thereby **worked out his own salvation**, and also **set an example as to the way and the means** whereby all men may be saved" (*The Mortal Messiah*, vol. 4, p. 434).

What about hell? It's not forever:

> Joseph Fielding Smith again: "Those who live lives of wickedness **may also be heirs of salvation**, that is, they too **shall be redeemed from death and from hell eventually**" (*Doctrines of Salvation*, vol. 2, p. 133).[19]

You are told to believe in Christ, that is, his atonement, but that alone isn't going to save you. You've got to "man up" and obey various requirements and also live a life of "good works." Like the Jesus presented in Catholicism, the work of the "Jesus Christ" of Mormonism is not enough to save you or guarantee you eternal life. What he was unable to DO you must DO the old-fashioned way . . . you must earn it.

In summary, you may not be at risk of hell (long term) and you're loaded up with lots of stuff to DO. But I keep wondering, how can you ever be sure when you've DONE enough?

Now, you may have noticed that each of these religions talks about Jesus, but . . .

What About Religions That
Don't Include **Jesus?**

WHAT IF YOU'RE
JEWISH?

Remember the list we saw under the Roman Catholic/ Protestant/Orthodox sections in the previous chapter? If you are Jewish, you have to keep 613 *mitzvot* (commandments) including the Ten Commandments outlined in the Scriptures.[1]

Whether one is Conservative, Orthodox, Reformed (among several others), all Jews highly value the *mitzvah,* which is a *good deed.* It's interwoven into the culture. There are many well-known Jewish philanthropists like TV and film actor Paul Newman, who co-founded a food company called Newman's Own. Newman donated all post-tax profits and royalties to charity. As of June 2012, these donations exceeded $330 million.[2]

Notable converts to Judaism include actress Marilyn Monroe and British-American actress Elizabeth Taylor.

According to an article in Reformed Judaism Online, Monroe converted just hours before she married playwright Arthur Miller on July 1, 1956. Taylor converted to Judaism at the age of 27 and was a lifelong supporter of the nation of Israel.[3]

Rabbinic **Judaism** teaches that good deeds and a life of Torah lead to reward in the afterlife.

But what better source can we examine about life after death than the Jewish Scriptures? The book of Daniel is particularly revealing . . .

> And many of them that sleep in the dust of the earth shall awake, some to everlasting life, and some to shame *and* everlasting contempt.[4]

And what about this?

> I said in mine heart, God shall judge the righteous and the wicked: for *there is* a time there for every purpose and for every work.[5]

So, according to the Jewish Scriptures, there will be

**A resurrection from the dead
and a judgment to come.**

Whatever you believe about Jesus of Nazareth, he was called a Rabbi by some of the Jews of his day. Many Jewish folks today still recognize him as a great teacher.

One day a lawyer approached Jesus and asked:

> Master, what shall I do to inherit eternal life? He said unto him, What is written in the law? how readest thou? And he answering said, Thou shalt love the Lord thy God with all thy heart, and with all thy soul, and with all thy strength, and with all thy mind; and thy neighbor as thyself. And he said unto him, Thou hast answered right: this do, and thou shalt live.[6]

And where did the lawyer get his information? Right from his own Scriptures in Deuteronomy 6:4–5. It's called the *Shema*.

THE SHEMA

The *Shema* is an affirmation of Judaism and a declaration of faith in one God. The obligation to recite the *Shema* is separate from the obligation to pray, and a Jew is obligated to say *Shema* in the morning and at night:[7]

> Hear, O Israel: The Lord our God is one Lord: And thou shalt love the Lord thy God with all thine heart, and with all thy soul, and with all thy might.[8]

The Jewish lawyer answered correctly. He clearly knew what he was commanded to DO in order to inherit eternal life.

That's what you must DO according to the Jewish Scriptures. Problem: Do you know anybody who has DONE what that Scripture says? Who has loved the Lord God with all their heart, soul, and strength? I haven't, have you?

Let's look at another very popular religion.

What If You're Muslim?

The Muslim religion is known as **Islam** and has more than one billion followers.

Many famous people have converted to Islam: singer-songwriter Cat Stevens, former World Heavyweight Champion Boxer Muhammad Ali, and former professional basketball players Kareem Abdul-Jabbar and Shaquille O'Neal.

Islam includes many different sects with variable beliefs. But if you were raised in this faith, then you're familiar with some basic tenets that are true for most Muslims.

THE SEVEN PRINCIPLES OF MUSLIM RELIGIOUS BELIEFS[9]

1. **The Unity of God** (*Tawheed*)
2. **Belief that Muhammad was the voice of God** (*Risallah*)
3. **Belief that angels exist** (*Mala 'ikah*)
4. **Trust and belief in the books of God** (*Kutubullah*)
5. **An understanding there will be a day of judgment** (*Yawmuddin*)
6. **Belief in predestination** (*Al-Qadr*)
7. **Belief that there is life after death** (*Akriah*)

We've already briefly looked at the Five Pillars of Wisdom, also known as the Five Pillars of Islam. Here they are again with a little more detail . . .

THE FIVE PILLARS OF ISLAM

DO these and you will please Allah:

1. **Testimony of Faith (*Kalima* [the shahada]):** A Muslim must be ready and willing to testify of their belief in Allah.

2. **Prayer (*Salat*):** Muslims follow a strict prayer schedule and must stop to pray at the appointed times each day.

3. **Almsgiving (*Zakat*):** Giving to those who are less fortunate is an important part of Muslim religion beliefs.

4. **Fasting (*Sawm*):** Regular fasts are believed to help bring Muslims under the submission of their God.

5. **Pilgrimage (*Hajj*):** This refers to a pilgrimage to Mecca, and is something every Muslim is to try and do at least one time.

Unfortunately, Muslim people have been painted with a broad brush and demonized as terrorists. The folks who do this sometimes have

an agenda and sometimes they're just ignorant. Plus, they must not know any Muslims, because many are very nice and hospitable people.

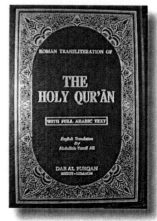

Allahu Akbar is a common Islamic Arabic expression meaning "God is great." If you're a Muslim, then you know it's used in various contexts––in prayer, as an expression of faith, in times of distress or victory, and to express defiance. Allah is God and Mohammed is his prophet.

It's important to clarify one point here: The Qur'an teaches that Allah does not have a son, but the Bible teaches that God has a son, Jesus Christ.[10] This means that the God of the Qur'an (known as Allah) is not the same as the God of the Bible (known as Jehovah.)

As a Muslim, you were taught that on the Last Day every man will account for what he has done and his eternal existence will be determined on that basis.

> And we have made every man's actions to cling to his neck, and we will bring forth to him on the resurrection day a book which he will find wide open.[11]

> Each man will be judged according to his situation, and every man who lives according to the truth to the best of his abilities will **achieve heaven**.[12]

What follows is from ShariahProgram.ca, a website that

> seeks to aid Muslims in choosing the clear, straight path which will lead them to the eternal destination of endless bliss (Paradise), Insha-Allah [Allah willing]. This life is a journey which presents to the traveller many paths. But there is only one clear, straight and correct path. Shariah in Arabic means the clear, well-trodden path to water . . . Just as water is vital to the life of human beings, likewise the implementation of Shariah in our day-to-day lives is the means of life for minds and souls.[13]

The writer clearly says the way to paradise (eternal life) is through faith plus good works. Sound familiar? The list of DOs looks very similar to the Roman Catholic requirements to save your soul. It's worth taking a look at this somewhat lengthy list:

> By increasing our acts of worship, and remembrance of Allah we will leave off sin and help safeguard ourselves from a Fire, the fuel of which is men and stones.

We Should Also Strive to:

> Protect our minds from thoughts, which are evil, because evil actions begin with evil thoughts.

> Protect our eyes by lowering our gazes and not looking at forbidden things.

> Protect our ears from lewd or evil speech where there is sin. We should also avoid listening to lies, gossip, music, slander, or blasphemy.

> Protect our tongues by saying always what is correct and true, and keeping it moist with the remembrance of Allah,

and keeping away from backbiting and other evil speech.

Protect our stomachs by eating the halal [foods permissible under Islamic law] and keeping away from the haram [*sic*; haraam are foods not permissible]. We should beware of eating usury, carrion, and swine or drinking intoxicants or taking drugs.

Protect our hands from taking what does not belong to us, or from doing harm to another Muslim.

Protect our legs from taking us to evil and corruption and an ultimate doom.

Protect our private parts from unlawful sexual intercourse.

Protect our wealth by not squandering it or holding on to it too tightly.

Protect our oaths, witnesses and trusts by not breaching or breaking a contract or pledge knowingly. We should not exceed our agreements, testify to falsehood or break our trusts.

Protect our families and children by keeping them away from the things that may be harmful and that may corrupt their minds and their souls.

Now, it is true that only Allah knows who the believers are, but that should not stop us from striving to be among their numbers. For the believers will have eternal bliss and complete success, because of the things that they did in this life. Allah says, "So no soul knows the delight of the eyes which is hidden for them; a reward for what they did." (Qur'an 32:17)

We now stand at the start of the race, so let us run forward quickly to the finish line, where the gates of Paradise will be open **for those who strive as they should**. The Messenger of Allah, sallallahu alayhe wa sallam [peace be upon Him], who said, "Paradise is surrounded by hardship and the Hellfire is surround by wishes and desires," has described the road to eternal bliss. (*Sahih al-Jami*)[14]

So it's a "race." You have to "strive as you should." But you can never be sure when or if you've DONE enough.

Like other religions, you need to (1) have faith, and (2) keep the moral law. But even if you DO these things, you still have no assurance you will get into paradise, because in the end, it's up to Allah to choose. Some he forgives, some he doesn't.

> To Allah belongs whatever is in the heavens and whatever is in the earth. Whether you show what is within yourselves or conceal it, Allah will bring you to account for it. Then He will forgive whom He wills and punish whom He wills, and Allah is over all things competent.[15]

> But those who disbelieve say, "The Hour will not come to us." Say, "Yes, by my Lord, it will surely come to you. [Allah is] the Knower of the unseen." Not absent from Him is an atom's weight within the heavens or within the earth or [what is] smaller than that or greater, except that it is in a clear register—That He may reward those who believe and do righteous deeds. Those will have forgiveness and noble provision. But those who

> strive against Our verses [seeking] to cause failure—for them will be a painful punishment of foul nature.[16]

Notice that he rewards those who (1) believe, and (2) DO righteous deeds. But how will you know when you've DONE enough? Unfortunately . . .

You don't find out till it's too late . . .

> And We place the scales of justice for the Day of Resurrection, so no soul will be treated unjustly at all. And if there is [even] the weight of a mustard seed, We will bring it forth. And sufficient are We as accountant.[17]

Islam eventually brings you back to the old "scales of justice" program; the same place as all the other religions including many Protestant denominations.

Most folks who don't follow any particular religion default to this position too. They figure if there's going to be a judgment, then good deeds are weighed against bad

The scales of justice

deeds. Interestingly, most folks figure it will go well with them. They're confident their good deeds will outweigh their bad deeds.

That's a nice thought, but I'm not sure they've really thought that one through. You'll see what I mean shortly. First, let's look at three of the main religions of the Far East.

What If You're Hindu?

Maharishi Mahesh Yogi, the Beatles, the *White Album*, and Hinduism

Most of the songs on *The White Album* were conceived during a transcendental meditation course with Maharishi ("great seer") Mahesh Yogi in India during the spring of 1968. The trip never brought peace to the group. "The Fab Four" disintegrated by the spring of 1970.

George Harrison's first single as a solo artist was released in 1970.[18] *My Sweet Lord* praised some of the main gods of Hinduism—like Brahma, Rama,

Vishnu, and Krishna—whom he referred to as "Lord." Harrison, like actress Julia Roberts, converted from Christianity to Hinduism.

Let's examine their choice.

SALVATION AND REINCARNATION

Salvation is the ability to escape from an endless cycle of birth, death, and rebirth. Most **Hindus** figure that they have many incarnations ahead of them before they can find salvation.

What you do in this life determines your position in the next.

For the Hindu, there is no future heaven or hell.

Your present suffering and bad fortune in this life is your hell—and it's a direct result of your karma in your past life. You are paying the price now for the evil you did in your past life.

Worse, if you don't DO your Karma just right in this life, you will be reincarnated into a lesser being or a lesser caste person in the next. What's even more tragic is that you can never know when you have DONE enough to merit an upgrade in the next life.

This is one tough religion. Maybe the Beatles should have stuck with the Church of England.

Hinduism is an attempt to "beat the game." By doing various works and performing rituals, you can escape the merry-go-round of death and re-birth. According to Hinduism there are . . .

Four Ways to Attain Salvation and Become One with God

Moksha (salvation) is when you achieve enlightenment and break free from the birth-death-rebirth cycle. When you reach this level of enlightenment, you enter a state of completeness and become one with God.

There are four ways to Moksha:

1. **The Way of Action:** This involves carrying out certain religious ceremonies, duties and rites. The objective is to perform works without regard for personal gain.

2. **The Way of Knowledge:** This requires using your mind and philosophy to come to a complete comprehension of the universe.

3. **The Way of Devotion:** Salvation is reached through acts of worship, based upon the love for a God (there are thousands of gods in Hinduism).

4. **The Royal Road:** The use of meditation and yoga techniques. This method of reaching salvation is typically only used by wandering monks.[19]

Once again we see that salvation is achieved by what you DO. It's all your effort.

Did somebody ever tell you that all religions teach the same thing and that there are many ways to God? That must have been their opinion, because it certainly isn't based on the facts.

But let's move on . . .

What If You're a Sikh?

Everybody wants a Guru.

People use the word "guru" (meaning *teacher*) all the time to describe someone who has all the answers. "Sikh" means disciple.

If you are from the State of Punjab in Northwest India, you most likely have a Sikh background. Sikhism is the fifth largest organized religion in the world with approximately 30 million adherents.

It was founded in the 15th century by a guru named Nanak Dev Ji. Born a Hindu, he concluded "God is neither Hindu nor Muslim and the path which I follow is God's."[20]

Sikhs are conspicuous by their headgear and dress.

The Sikhs have some pretty nice beliefs. For example, Sikhs believe that no matter what race, sex, or religion one is, all are equal in God's eyes. Men and women are equal and share the same rights, and women can lead in prayers. Plus Guru Nanak stressed that a Sikh should balance work, worship, and charity, and should defend the rights of all creatures, and in particular, fellow human beings.[21] Who's not in favor of that?

But here comes the rest of the story.

A Sikh believes in reincarnation. Like Hindus and Buddhists, Sikhs believe that deeds done in this life will determine your station in the next. You will take birth again and again until you attain salvation by becoming One with God.[22]

> In order to **attain** salvation one must live a honest life and meditate on God. Sikhism shows the way to attain salvation and become One with God. Sikhism instructs that you do not have to fast, abstain, go on renunciation or enter a monastery in order to meet God. All you have to do is **have faith**, **recite** the Name of God [which is "Truth"] and **remember** Him for each possible moment.[23]

Note that salvation must be "attained." Plus you are to "remember Him for each possible moment."

What if you skip some moments? How do you make up for lost time?

And it gets even scarier.

You never know if you have DONE enough to escape the cycle of death and rebirth. Take a look at this:

> Bhagat Trilochan, an author of Guru Granth Sahib Scripture writes on the subject of afterlife, that at the time of death **the final thought determines** how one reincarnates.[24]

So it comes down to the bottom of the ninth inning with two outs and a three and two count. Everything rides on the last pitch. That's hardly any assurance of anything.

And what does this religion promise if you follow it? Nothing more than escape from the treadmill of rebirth. Then you lose your own identity as you are absorbed into God.

We've got one more major religion to look at . . .

What If You're a Buddhist?

Buddha means "enlightened one"; his former name was Siddhartha. He was a young prince who was sad to see death so he left the palace and began to live an ordinary person's life and sought the answers to pain, suffering, sickness, and death. After many days of meditating under a Banyan (fig) tree, he got an answer and people called him Buddha, the enlightened one.

It's been estimated that there are over one billion Buddhists. Notable converts to this religion include actor Richard Gere, singer-songwriter David Bowie, actor Steven Seagal, and actresses Sharon Stone and Kate Bosworth.

If you were brought up in **Buddhism**, then you know what's required of you. Buddha taught . . .

The Four Noble Truths

1. All in the world is sorrow and suffering.
2. Craving causes suffering.
3. Ending craving means you end suffering.
4. The way to end craving is to follow . . .

The Eightfold Path

1. Have right views.
2. Have right resolve.
3. Practice right speech.
4. Practice right conduct.
5. Have right livelihood.
6. Have right effort.
7. Have right mindfulness.
8. Have right concentration.

Buddha decreed a path of spiritual improvement based on the acceptance of the Four Noble Truths and on such things as avoidance of ill will, malicious talk, lust, and hurting living things.[25]

And what do you get in the end? If you're successful (and nothing says you will be, because you don't know who judges how well you followed the Eightfold Path), here's what you get . . .

Nothingness.
That's what Nirvana is . . .

Like the Hindus, Buddhists want to escape the wheel of rebirth. They seek to obtain Nirvana (literally "Bow Out") and become one with the universe. Most Hindus believe that Brahman is the universe.

Buddhist beliefs could best be summed up in this quotation from one of their scriptures:

> By oneself, indeed, is evil done; by oneself is one defiled. By oneself is evil left undone; by oneself, indeed, is one purified. Purity and impurity depend on oneself. No one purifies another.[26]

How's that for working yourself clean from sin? The point is that all religions tell you what to DO, but they never tell you when you've DONE enough.

Anyway, it sounds like a lot of work to gain nothingness in the end, doesn't it?

It's fascinating how millions follow the Buddha's teachings yet . . .

Buddha never rose from the dead.

Speaking of rising from the dead . . .

Isn't that the hope of every man that lives? That somehow "you" won't really "die"? We all want to live forever. Nobody wants to cease to exist. Of course, many people want to escape the misery and heartache that comes with this life (that's why they opt for suicide), but what we all really want is a better life.

What if you could get (1) a better life now and (2) a far better life in the future that includes life after death, plus (3) lose your fear of death and (4) have all this given to you as a free gift? That's coming up soon.

But first, how about considering what the Bible says? It's a pretty controversial book, so let's start by finding out what people say about it . . .

4

What People Say
About the Bible

The Bible is the most loved, hated, reverenced, and ridiculed book on earth.

The "Good Book" is so precious to some folks that they've sacrificed their lives to translate, print, distribute, and even just own it. Others have spent their lives trying to prove that it's nothing more than a book of myth and superstition.

Some people praise the Bible . . .

Thomas Jefferson (1743-1826)

You know him as one of America's Founding Fathers, the main author of the Declaration of Independence, and the third President of the United States.[1]

You've seen his image hundreds of times, especially when you were a kid. That's because **Thomas Jefferson**'s face has been on the nickel since 1938.

Here's what Jefferson said about the Bible:

> **A studious perusal of the sacred volume will make better citizens, better fathers, and better husbands.**[2]

Helen Keller (1880-1968)

If you've read the play or seen the film, you know **Helen Keller** from *The Miracle Worker*. It depicts how Keller's teacher, Annie Sullivan, "broke through the isolation imposed by a near complete lack of language, allowing the girl to blossom as she learned to communicate." Keller became an author, political activist, and popular lecturer, as well as the first deaf-blind person to earn a Bachelor of Arts degree.[3]

She wrote:

> **The BIBLE gives me a deep, comforting sense that "things seen are temporal, and things unseen are eternal."**[4]

PATRICK HENRY
(1736–1799)

We may not remember all we learned about him in school, but who doesn't remember **Patrick Henry**'s famous line, "Give me Liberty, or give me Death!" Henry was an attorney, politician, and Founding Father who became known as an orator during the movement for independence in Virginia in the 1770s.

He said this about the Bible:

> **There is a Book worth all other books
> which were ever printed.**[5]

DANIEL WEBSTER
(1782-1852)

Daniel Webster was an important American statesman and senator from Massachusetts prior to the Civil War. We may not think about him much today, but Webster was selected as one of the "five greatest U.S. Senators" by a Senate Committee in 1957.[6]

He said these words about the Bible:

> **The BIBLE fits man for life and prepares him for death.**
>
> **Education is useless without the BIBLE.**

NOAH WEBSTER (1758–1843)

Remember all those spelling tests in school? **Noah Webster** gets the credit for that. He was "a lexicographer, textbook pioneer, English-language spelling reformer, political writer, editor, and prolific author." His many achievements earned him the title "Father of American Scholarship and Education." Five generations of American children learned how to spell and read from Webster's *Elementary Spelling Book*, known as "the blue-backed speller."[7]

And, of course, he is probably best known for his *Dictionary of the American Language*.

Webster was quite a guy. It's said of Webster that he "taught millions to read but not one to sin." Here are a couple of things he said about the Bible:

> **The Bible is the Book of faith, and a Book of doctrine, and a Book of morals, and a Book of religion, of special revelation from God; but it is also a Book which teaches man its responsibility, his own dignity, and his equality with his fellow man.**

> **The BIBLE is the chief moral cause of all that is good, and the best corrector of all that is evil, in human society; the best Book for regulating temporal concerns of men, and the only Book that can serve as an infallible guide to future felicity.**[8]

Some people ridicule the Bible . . .

Richard Dawkins
(b. 1941)

Richard Dawkins is a famous atheist and author of *The God Delusion*. He got his head handed to him by Ben Stein in Stein's highly controversial Intelligent Design documentary titled *Expelled: No Intelligence Allowed*. While unwilling to admit that life has to have a supernatural explanation, Dawkins notes that perhaps life was delivered to our planet by highly evolved aliens.

Look at this exchange between Dawkins and Stein:

> <u>Ben Stein</u>: What do [you] think is the possibility that intelligent design might turn out to

be the answer to some issues in genetics . . . or in evolution?

Richard Dawkins: Well . . . it could come about in the following way: it could be that uh, at some earlier time somewhere in the universe a civilization evolved . . . probably by some kind of Darwinian means to a very, very high level of technology and designed a form of life that they seeded onto . . . perhaps this . . . this planet. Um, now that is a possibility. And uh, an intriguing possibility. And I suppose it's possible that you might find evidence for that if you look at the um, at the detail . . . details of our chemistry molecular biology you might find a signature of some sort of designer.

Ben Stein: [voice over] Wait a second. Richard Dawkins thought intelligent design might be a legitimate pursuit?

Richard Dawkins: Um, and that designer could well be a higher intelligence from elsewhere in the universe. But that higher intelligence would itself would have to come about by some explicable or ultimately explicable process. It couldn't have just jumped into existence spontaneously. That's the point.

<u>Ben Stein</u>: [voice over] So professor Dawkins was not against intelligent design, just certain types of designers. Such as God.[9]

Dawkins is an *a* • *theist*—*a* meaning "no" and *theos* meaning "God." And yet he believes that "a higher intelligence" could exist that is self-sustaining and didn't evolve (i.e., "couldn't have just jumped into existence spontaneously").

Maybe he just should have lied. After all, if there is no God and death is final, what difference does it make?

Anyway, here's what Dawkins says about the Bible:

> **To be fair, much of the Bible is not systematically evil but just plain weird, as you would expect of a chaotically cobbled-together anthology of disjointed documents, composed, revised, translated, distorted and "improved" by hundreds of anonymous authors, editors and copyists, unknown to us and mostly unknown to each other, spanning nine centuries.[10]**

ALEISTER CROWLEY (1875–1947)

Here's a guy you probably aren't too familiar with. **Aleister Crowley** is widely thought of as the most influential occultist of all time. "Crowley was also bisexual, a recreational drug experimenter and a social critic." As you might imagine, he revolted against established moral and religious values of his day, promoting a "Do What Thou Wilt" philosophy. He was certainly notorious; in fact, the popular press denounced him as "the wickedest man in the world."[11]

Guitarist Jimmy Page of Led Zeppelin purchased Crowley's former home in Loch Ness, Scotland, in 1971 and in 1975 told *Rolling Stone* it was haunted, though he didn't blame Crowley. "It was also a church that was burned to the ground with the congregation in it. Strange things have happened in that house that had nothing to do with Crowley. The bad vibes were already there. A man was beheaded there, and sometimes you can hear his head rolling down."[12]

A tour of Crowley's place might make a good episode of *Ghost Stories*. Here's Crowley's opinion of the Bible:

One would go mad if one took the Bible seriously; but to take it seriously one must be already mad.[13]

Isaac Asimov
(1920–1992)

Besides being a biochemistry professor at Boston University, **Isaac Asimov** was a prolific writer and is best known for his science fiction works, such as the *Foundation Series*, and for his popular science books.

A few years before his death, Asimov wrote, "If I were not an atheist, I would believe in a God who would choose to save people on the basis of the totality of their lives and not the pattern of their words."

His God turns out to be very much like the Gods of all religions: Salvation is a do-it-yourself program based on good works outweighing bad.

He also believed that hell is "'the drooling dream of a sadist' crudely affixed to an all-merciful God":[14]

... if even human governments were willing to curtail cruel and unusual punishments, wondered Asimov, why would punishment in the afterlife not be restricted to a limited term? Asimov rejected the idea that a human belief or action could merit infinite punishment. If an afterlife existed, he claimed, the longest and most severe punishment would be reserved for those who "slandered God by inventing Hell."[15]

He did a lot of deep thinking. But what was he like at home?

Particularly in his later years, Asimov to some extent cultivated an image of himself as an amiable lecher. In 1971, as a response to the popularity of sexual guidebooks such as *The Sensuous Woman* (by "J") and *The Sensuous Man* (by "M"), Asimov published *The Sensuous Dirty Old Man* under the byline "Dr. 'A'" (although his full name was printed on the paperback edition, first published 1972).[16]

A lecher is a person with feelings that are lustful or sexual in an extreme or unnatural way. For a smart man, that's kind of creepy, no? Anyway, here is one of his comments on the Bible.

> **Properly read, the Bible is the most potent force for atheism ever conceived.**[17]

SAMUEL LANGHORNE CLEMENS (1835-1910)

You know this American author and humorist as **Mark Twain**, author of *The Adventures of Tom Sawyer* and its sequel, *Adventures of Huckleberry Finn*. "Twain generally avoided publishing his most heretical opinions on religion in his lifetime," but we know them from essays and stories published later.[18]

Twain stated that he believed in an almighty God, but not in any messages, revelations, holy scriptures such as the Bible, Providence, or retribution in the afterlife . . . In some later writings in the 1890s, he was less optimistic about the goodness of

God, observing that "if our Maker *is* all-powerful for good or evil, He is not in His right mind."

At other times, he conjectured sardonically that perhaps God had created the world with all its tortures for some purpose of His own, but was otherwise indifferent to humanity, which was too petty and insignificant to deserve His attention anyway . . . Those who knew Twain well late in life recount that he dwelt on the subject of the afterlife, his daughter Clara saying: "Sometimes he believed death ended everything, but most of the time he felt sure of a life beyond."[19]

It's pretty clear, Mark Twain was unsettled about life after death. Maybe that's why he said this about the Bible:

> **The Bible has noble poetry in it . . . and some good morals and a wealth of obscenity, and upwards of a thousand lies.**[20]

Kind of an odd comment, but that's Mark Twain.

Although here's something he said that's really profound:

> **It's easier to fool people than to convince them that they have been fooled.**[21]

The Bible really polarizes people, doesn't it?

Now, these are all interesting comments from interesting people, but the comments are just their opinions. You've got a serious problem to solve. You **must** know for sure what happens after you die in order to get rid of your fear of death. But you need reliable information.

Here's a thought; why not consider . . .

What the **Bible** Says

Why not consider what the Bible says about the afterlife? After all, the Bible is truly a remarkable book. It's been banned by many governments over the centuries, so whatever is in it must be a threat to someone's state-sponsored religion.

More importantly, the Bible actually gives you a view of life after death found nowhere else. This book centers on a man (actually the God man Jesus Christ) who is the only one qualified to deliver accurate information to you on the afterlife. That's because history and Scripture both tell us that he rose from the dead. So . . .

Why not get the facts from someone who's actually died and come back?

Surely he's the most qualified person to get information from regarding the afterlife. And since the Bible is his book, then it's the most authoritative source of his testimony.

Jesus' death and resurrection is critical because your fear of death is never going to leave you if it's not true. In the history of religious leaders, he's the only one who's been documented to have risen from the dead. Muhammad is still dead, and so is Buddha.

Any hope we have hinges on his resurrection from the dead. Like it says in the Scripture . . .

> And if Christ be not raised, your faith *is* vain; ye are yet in your sins. Then they also which are fallen asleep [died] in Christ are perished.[1]

It's no wonder the resurrection is called into question. For example, if you are a Muslim, then you are taught that in the Qur'an Jesus was not crucified, but was raised bodily to heaven by God.

That they said (in boast), "We killed Christ Jesus the son of Mary, the Messenger of Allah"; but they killed him not, nor crucified him, but so it was made to appear to them, and those who differ therein are full of doubts, with no (certain) knowledge, but only conjecture to follow, for of a surety they killed him not: Nay, Allah raised him up unto Himself; and Allah is Exalted in Power, Wise.[2]

It's also interesting to note that the Qur'an just said that Allah raised Jesus up to himself. Why would he bother doing that? Anyway, back to the crucifixion . . .

Muslim scholars offer four positions:[3]

1. Jesus' crucifixion did not last long enough for him to die (minority view).

2. God gave someone (i.e., Judas) Jesus' appearance, causing everyone to believe that Jesus was crucified (majority view).

3. Jesus was nailed to a cross, but as his body is immortal, he did not "die" or was not "crucified" [to death]; it only appeared so.

4. Since God does not use deceit, therefore they contend that the crucifixion just did not occur.

If you were brought up in Judaism or Islam, one thing **can't** be true—that Jesus really died and rose again under his own power. Because if he did, then (1) he is more than a prophet, (2) his claim to deity must be true, and (3) he is indeed the Messiah, the savior of the world. All three of these positions are denied by both of these religions.

According to the Bible, (1) Jesus claimed to be the Christ (Messiah), (2) predicted his own resurrection from the dead, and (3) finally actually did rise three days after being pronounced dead by the Jewish leaders. Here's what they said . . .

> Now the next day, that followed the day of the preparation, the chief priests and Pharisees came together unto Pilate Saying, Sir, we remember that that deceiver said, **while he was yet alive**, After three days I will rise again.[4]

The leaders also knew he rose from the dead because they paid off the watchmen who witnessed the event at the tomb . . .

> Now when they were going, behold, some of the watch came into the city,

and shewed unto the chief priests all the things that were done. And when they were assembled with the elders, and had taken counsel, they gave large money unto the soldiers, Saying, Say ye, His disciples came by night, and stole him away while we slept. And if this come to the governor's ears, we will persuade him, and secure you. So they took the money, and did as they were taught: and this saying is commonly reported among the Jews until this day.[5]

Jesus was a threat to the priests, elders, and leaders. If it became known that he rose from the dead, the fear was that all men would believe on him: and the Romans would come and take away their positions and power. Paying cash to shut up the guards was a worthwhile investment.

The point is that Jesus did rise from the dead and is alive right now.

But I'm getting ahead of myself . . .

The book about Jesus Christ is the Bible, and it's different from all other books on earth.

THE SOURCE OF THE INFORMATION

I am convinced (to the point where I'd stake my life on it) that the Bible is absolutely true. Thirty-five years ago, I wasn't. I thought it was just a collection of myths and fables.

The Word of our God shall stand for ever Isaiah 40:8

However, after reading it 17 times from cover to cover and studying in and about it for literally thousands of hours, I am sure that it is true, accurate, and factual. And I take it literally where I can.

I've taught the Bible to preschool kids through adults. My home library consists of several hundred Bible-related volumes including books by guys who don't believe in it. I know how we got it, including which major Greek and Hebrew manuscripts were involved in the transmission of the text.

I am familiar with the principal Greek New Testament printed texts, as well as how the various English translations compare with each other. I even wrote a book on Bible versions called *Which Bible Would Jesus Use? The Bible Version Controversy Explained and Resolved.*

I mention these things only because I want you to know that I am familiar with the Book and its contents.

Let me give you a few reasons why I believe the Bible is . . .

The only true and accurate record of historical facts on the face of the earth.

God wrote the Bible using more than 40 men on 3 continents over the space of about 1,600 years. Yet, there is a planned design in the Book that runs throughout all those years without any writer knowing it. It's unlike any other religious book on the planet, including all of the Muslim, Hindu, and Buddhist writings, in that it quotes the Creator speaking about Himself, as the Creator.

You find "Thus saith the Lord," or "the LORD spake," or "the LORD said," or "the LORD hath spoken," over 800 times.

But . . .

You know what really impresses me about the Bible?

It's not so much its miraculous mathematical preciseness—the chances of the 48 Old Testament prophecies about Jesus Christ (some were written up to 1,400 years before he was born) being fulfilled to the letter has been estimated at 1 in 10^{157}.

It's not even the fact that after 19 centuries of trying, no one has been able to prove even one historical or scientific error in either Testament. I say this after having been a believer in the Big Bang, the Theory of Evolution, Neanderthal man, and so on. I had faith in all these things.

What a surprise when I found out that there are no real facts to support them. But that's another subject.

The one thing that really impresses me about the Bible is what it says about God's character. The Creator of the universe has gone on record as stating that there is something he not only will not do but something he cannot do. In fact, something that is impossible for him to do.

That one thing is . . .

8-6-15

God can't lie!

God is not a man, **that he should lie** . . . And also the Strength of Israel **will not lie** nor repent . . . **God, that cannot lie**, . . . **it was impossible for God to lie.**[6]

Take it to heart; the Lord . . .

Should not

    Will not

        Cannot

            Lie.

                It's impossible for him to lie.

You will **never** get over your fear of death unto you have a good **reason why** you don't need to be afraid anymore.

But . . .

You need trustworthy information about death and beyond.

And you can only get it from someone who is honest and worthy of your trust, and more importantly, someone who has actually gone through the experience. That person is the Lord Jesus Christ.

He won't lie to you or deceive you. He always has told the truth and always will tell a truth. The written record he has given to you is the Bible. The book is true because the God who "wrote" it is true.

And like the Scripture says:

Buy the truth, and sell it not.[7]

The Bible says two very important things about what happens after death. The first is . . .

There is a Judgment coming.

The Bible says:

> It is appointed unto men once to die, but after this **the judgment**.[8]

As you probably suspected, there's a judgment coming. Most of the religions we looked at also teach this. And when you think of all the nasty people and injustice in the world, who could be against that? The problem is that the verse says that judgment is for "men." That means you and me.

And if this is true, then you'd better be ready. The rest of this report will show you what the Bible says about:

- How to be ready for the coming judgment (no matter what you've done in the past),

- How to get eternal life right now and know for sure that you've got it, and finally,

- Why you can never lose your eternal life.

Here's the thing . . .

Once you learn the truth about death and beyond and take appropriate action . . .

You'll never need to fear the prospect of death again.

I don't. And neither will you if you just keep reading. Before I go on, let me say that I am not looking forward to the "process" of dying (by accident, sickness, etc.)—but my fear of the unknown is gone.

Just about everyone you talk to believes they're good enough to pass God's judgment. But after **actually reading** what the Bible **says**, I don't know **anybody** who is really "good enough" to make it.

Here's what I mean . . .

Even King David (who killed Goliath) said:

> Mine iniquities have taken hold upon me, so that I am not able to look up;

**they are more than the hairs of mine
head**: therefore my heart faileth me.[9]

Did you know that there is an average of about
120,000 hairs on a person's head? That means he
was admitting to in excess of 120,000 sins. Are we
any better than he?

As I got older and finished high school and
college, I soon realized that trying **not** to commit
a mortal sin was just about impossible. So I just
quit trying. By the time I graduated from college, I
doubted if God even existed. As the Scripture says,

**The fool hath said in his heart,
There is no God.[10]**

That was me. I was a fool. And I lived my life
that way.

I guess that it wasn't so much that I didn't
believe God existed but that I didn't **want** to be
accountable to him. I didn't want to face **Judgment
Day**. That's the day when everyone of us will come
face to face with the Lord Jesus Christ as he sits on
his throne and judges us. Like the Scripture says . . .

**For we must all appear
before the judgment seat of Christ.[11]**

But I'm getting ahead of myself . . .

Around 1976, after my mother had been diagnosed with cancer, I really started to question whether or not there was life after death. Up to that point, I was pretty well resigned to the belief that when you died, you were dead, The End.

Even so, I really wanted to be sure . . .

MY SEARCH FOR TRUTH

I started to read books on death and dying (i.e., Elisabeth Kübler-Ross, etc.). I investigated things such as *Rosicrucianism*, *Eckankar* (including soul travel), *Spiritism*, *Reincarnation* and *Regressive Hypnosis*.

For a while I believed that God was a Universal Mind that you could tap into for success. I read books on the subject. The parallel today is the book *The Secret*. Promoted heavily by Oprah Winfrey, it talks about the "Law of Attraction" in which a "universal force" is available that can be harnessed for the betterment of our lives.

I almost bought into reincarnation for a while, because I had always believed in ghosts and regressive hypnosis. However, after some months of further research, I concluded that it just didn't ring true.

All I really wanted to know was the truth. What happens to you after you die? What is the secret of life and death?

I used to listen to a man on the radio who taught things out of the Bible. I knew Bible stories and I sure knew the Catholic religion. But I learned some things that the Bible said that no one had ever told me before.

A second very important thing the Bible says about what happens after death is that . . .

There is a literal heaven and a literal hell.

I wish it weren't so, but according to the Bible, hell is located in "the heart of the earth."[12]

That's about 4,000 miles straight down under your feet—and yes, according to the Bible it does contain unquenchable fire.

It's not that I wasn't taught about hell as a kid; it's just that I eventually (for obvious reasons) didn't believe anyone would go there except Hitler, Stalin, Mao, and the like. The truth about hell is that many, many real people (people you once knew) who once lived on the earth are now in the earth.

Actually, Jesus spoke more about hell than he did about heaven. Speaking of the Father, he said:

> But I will forewarn you whom ye shall fear: Fear him, which **after he hath killed hath power to cast into hell**; yea, I say unto you, Fear him.[13]

He also said:

> And if thy right eye offend thee, pluck it out, and cast it from thee: for it is profitable for thee that one of thy members should perish, **and not that thy whole body should be cast into hell.**[14]

Surprisingly, according to the Scripture and contrary to popular belief . . .

Most people end up going to hell instead of heaven.

But how can this be?

Because they expect to get to heaven by what they DO—by their good works outweighing the bad. Sadly, although many folks sincerely believe this, it turns out not to be true according to the Bible.

What a shocker. Why didn't anybody tell me this?

And you know what's really tragic? The reason most people end up in hell is because they never believed or never knew (a situation you won't face after reading this report) what God said about how to avoid hell.

Even religious people go to hell by following a "good works" DO-it-yourself way that we were all taught would get us to heaven. And yet the Scripture says:

There is a way which seemeth right unto a man, but the end thereof are the ways of death.[15]

I know it's hard to believe, but here are Jesus' own words about the fact that more people are lost forever in hell than are saved from it . . .

Enter ye in at the strait gate: for **wide** *is* the gate, and **broad *is* the way**, that **leadeth to destruction**, and **many** there be which **go in thereat**:

Because strait *is* the gate, and **narrow** *is* **the way**, which leadeth unto life, and **few** there be that **find it**.[16]

Incredibly, this happens in spite of all that God has already DONE to make sure it doesn't happen. There's more on that later, but first here's the rest of my story . . .

How **I** Finally **Lost** My **Fear** of **Death**

No one had to convince me that I was a wicked sinner. I broke every commandment short of killing someone. I certainly had not loved the LORD with all my heart, with all my soul, and with all my might. Therefore, I had continuously broken the first and greatest commandment, which is . . .

> **Thou shalt love the Lord thy God** with **all** thy heart, and with **all** thy soul, and with **all** thy mind. This is the first and great commandment.[1]

Now if anyone DOES keep this FIRST and GREAT commandment and all the other commandments, they would truly "earn" eternal life because they would be perfectly righteous.

And if you'd like to try,

Here are the works the Lord Jesus Christ said you must do to earn eternal life.

Remember the conversation Jesus had with the lawyer we read earlier?

> And, behold, a certain lawyer stood up, and tempted him, saying, Master, **what shall I do** to inherit eternal life?

> He said unto him, What is written in the law? how readest thou? And he answering said, **Thou shalt love the Lord thy God with all thy heart, and with all thy soul, and with all thy strength, and with all thy mind**; and thy neighbour as thyself.

> And he said unto him, Thou hast answered right: **this do, and thou shalt live.**[2]

Go ahead; **DO** this commandment if you can. If you DO it, according to the Lord Jesus Christ, you will live. Great.

The problem is, no one can **earn** eternal life in this manner for the simple reason that no one has ever kept even this first and great commandment, or for that matter, all the others.

I sure didn't. Have you?

Besides, God has already gone on record as stating:

> As it is written, **There is none righteous,** no, not one: There is **none** that understandeth, there is **none** that seeketh after God. They are **all** gone out of the way, they are together become unprofitable; **there is none that doeth good,** no, not one.[3]

God doesn't have a very high opinion of our righteousness. That being the case, I've got a confession to make. I broke all 10 of the Lord's commandments and then some. Here's what I mean . . .

I already described how I couldn't keep Commandment 1. How about Commandment 2?

> Thou shalt not make unto thee

> any graven image, or any likeness of
> any thing that is in heaven above, or
> that is in the earth beneath, or that
> is in the water under the earth: Thou
> shalt not bow down thyself to them,
> nor serve them: for I the Lord thy God
> **am a jealous God.**[4]

I never bowed down to any graven image, but no matter, the Scripture says in Colossians 3:5 that **covetousness . . . is idolatry** and I sure was covetous.

It also says **Stubbornness is as . . . idolatry.**[5]

Guilty again. And who isn't stubborn?

They say, "guilt is every man's hangman." Isn't it true? It sure was for me.

We don't worship little stone images in this culture. Our idols can be other people, houses, sports, jewelry, music, clothing, equipment, cars, or just about anything you give priority to instead of God. Anything or anybody I gave my heart to instead of God was my idol. Anyway, there went Commandment 2.

Commandment 3? I broke that one thousands of times.

> Thou shalt not take the name of the
> Lord thy God in vain; for **the Lord will**

not hold him guiltless that taketh his name in vain.[6]

For they speak against thee wickedly, and **thine enemies take thy name in vain.**[7]

I used to be in the construction business. I had a terribly filthy mouth—and quite frankly, a mind to match. I combined the name of the Lord Jesus Christ with the vilest language. It was terrible (as anyone I used to work with will attest).

Here's the thing, every time I blasphemed and used the name "God" or "Jesus" or "Jesus Christ" in vain as in the literally thousands of times I cursed, I made myself an "**enemy**" of God.

Who knew? Those are his words, not mine. And worse, God doesn't close his eyes to it. It will not go unpunished, for the Scripture says:

God is Angry with the Wicked
Every Day.
~ Psalm 7:11

It also says:

> God is jealous, and the Lord revengeth; the Lord revengeth, and is furious; the Lord will take vengeance on his adversaries, and he reserveth wrath for his enemies.[8]

> Thine hand shall **find out all thine enemies**: thy right hand shall find out those that hate thee. Thou shalt make them as a fiery oven in the time of thine anger: **the Lord shall swallow them up in his wrath, and the fire shall devour them**.[9]

Pretty serious, isn't it? And I was right in the path of the wrath of God and didn't even know it.

If you're guilty of this sin like I was, keep reading. There is hope. Later, you'll learn how to get complete and permanent forgiveness for all the times you transgressed this commandment, as well as for all the rest of the sins you've committed, or ever will commit.

But first, let's continue looking at the commandments.

I'm not Jewish, so keeping the Sabbath (Saturday) holy, Commandment 4, doesn't apply to me. However, sad to say, many times I did not honor my parents, thereby violating Commandment 5, which is . . .

📖 COMMANDMENT 5:
HONOUR THY FATHER AND THY MOTHER.[10]

And who do you know that hasn't dishonored their parents at one time or another? It's funny, but when you think of it, if what the Scripture says is true (and it is),

---

the wages of sin is death [11]

---

then not one of us would have ever made it out of our teen years. The fact that we are still alive is due to what the Bible calls God's "longsuffering."

> The Lord is not slack concerning his promise, as some men count slackness; but is **longsuffering** to us-ward, **not willing that any should perish**, but that all should come to repentance.[12]

📖 COMMANDMENT 6:
THOU SHALT NOT KILL.[13]

No, I never killed anyone. But I've sure done a number on other people's reputations with just plain idle gossip. Jesus said:

> But I say unto you, That **every idle word** that men shall speak, they shall give account thereof **in the day of judgment**.[14]

Imagine; you must give an account to the Lord Jesus Christ as he sits on a throne for **every idle word you ever spoke**. And this is after you've shot off your mouth for years saying all kinds of stupid things that you'd just as soon forget.

Scary isn't it? But there's more . . .

📖 COMMANDMENT 7:
THOU SHALT NOT COMMIT ADULTERY.[15]

By the way, Jesus said you're guilty of adultery even if you look on a woman to lust after her in your heart. Ouch. Or, for the ladies, how many times has your heart been fluttered by movie stars or men other than your husband?

📖 COMMANDMENT 8:
THOU SHALT NOT STEAL.[16]

📖 COMMANDMENT 9:
THOU SHALT NOT BEAR FALSE WITNESS
AGAINST THY NEIGHBOR.[17]

📖 COMMANDMENT 10:
THOU SHALT NOT COVET THY NEIGHBOR'S
HOUSE, THOU SHALT NOT COVET THY
NEIGHBOR'S WIFE, NOR HIS MANSERVANT,
NOR HIS MAIDSERVANT, NOR HIS OX, NOR
HIS ASS, NOR ANY THING THAT IS THY
NEIGHBOR'S.[18]

I was guilty of violating all these commandments too.

And not just a few times either. One thing the nuns taught me was the commandments. I knew I was a sinner and I deserved to go to hell.

And why not?

According to Scripture, taking God's name in vain made me his enemy, even if I broke no others.

Sure, I know, everyone says, "We're all sinners, God understands that." "Don't be so hard on yourself. Besides, God will forgive you if you just confess your sins to him."

But most folks don't realize . . .

Just confessing sins to God won't keep you out of hell.

That's like a criminal confessing his crime to the judge and getting off scot-free because he ad-

Only one hole will sink the boat!

mits his guilt and says he's sorry. You'd be outraged if a judge did that—and rightly so—because there is such a thing as justice.

When you appear before a judge, you're there because you've broken the law. The fact that you may be a "good person" and "tried not to hurt anybody" isn't the question.

What's worse is the Scripture says if you've broken one commandment you're guilty of all.

Why?

Because it only takes one sin to classify you as a sinner.

> For whosoever shall keep the whole
> law, and yet offend in one point, he
> is guilty of all.[19]

That has to be the worst verse in Scripture. Imagine; the Lord is telling you that if you just commit **one** sin—just **one**—you're as guilty as if you committed them all.

In short, one sin sinks your boat. That means we're all in the same fix. No one's going to get away with anything.

More importantly . . .

God is a righteous Judge.

There is a price to be paid for sinning against a Holy God. If there weren't, then God's promise to punish sinners would be a lie. And he says he will punish the wicked:

> The wicked shall be turned into hell.[20]

It's not a lie. God does not lie. And it's not a joke either. My problem was that I was a wicked man headed for hell. Being guilty, what could I give for a ransom for my soul? As the Scripture says . . .

None of them can by any means redeem his brother, nor give to God a ransom for him: (For **the redemption of their soul is precious.**)[21]

But here's the good news . . .

God provided a very precious **ransom** for my soul (and yours too).

Even as the Son of man came not to be ministered unto, but to minister, and **to give his life a ransom** for many.[22]

Christ Jesus came into the world **to save sinners.**[23]

The fact is that Jesus Christ took on himself ALL my filth and sin— and yours too.

But he was wounded for our transgressions, he was bruised for our iniquities . . . and the Lord hath laid on him the iniquity of us all.[24]

The Lord laid all my sins on Jesus and then punished him in my place. And he is the only one qualified to stand in my place because he never had any sins of his own to die for. Speaking of Jesus, the Scripture says that he **was in all points tempted like as we are, yet without sin.**[25]

I was the one who deserved to be punished—not him. He never sinned even once in his whole life.

Not only did the Lord lay all our sins on him, he actually made Jesus to BE sin for us.

> For he hath **made him to be sin** for us, **who knew no sin**; that we might be made the righteousness of God in him.[26]

When I was preparing this report, I asked a graphic artist to create something that would look like the illustration on the next page. She refused.

She said the subject matter was offensive. And it is. It's both shocking and offensive. And yet it depicts exactly what the Scripture says in graphic form.

If it had not been absolutely necessary, the Lord would not have done what he did. He would have found a better way to forgive and forget your sins.

As you stare at him on that cross, consider that God made Jesus to be sin for us.

God Made Jesus To Be Sin

"Christ (was) made a curse for us" Gal 3:13

"My God! My God! Why Hast Thou Forsaken Me?"

"Cursed is everyone that hangeth on a tree" Gal 3:13

I Owed A Debt
I Could Not Pay
He Paid A Debt
He Did Not Owe

Galatians 3:13 Christ hath redeemed us
from the curse of the law,
being made a curse for us:
for it is written,
Cursed [is] every one that hangeth on a tree:

Isaiah 53:6
... and the LORD hath laid on him
the iniquity of us all.

2 Corinthians 5:21
For he hath made him to be sin for us,
who knew no sin;
that we might be made
the righteousness of God in him

From the "God Made Jesus to Be Sin" tract by Michael Pearl. Published by No Greater Joy Ministries, www.nogreaterjoy.org. Used with permission.

The Lord Jesus Christ, who knew no sin, was made "to be sin for us." He took our sins upon himself. He bore our sins. But he was never a sinner himself.

It's no wonder that God can completely forgive sins and still be just. He did execute a guilty, vile criminal. I was the criminal, but the sinless Lord Jesus Christ voluntarily took all my sins on himself and suffered the wrath of God in my place.

And if you'll come to him, his execution can count for you too.

First, God poured out the cup of his wrath upon Jesus in my place. Then Jesus went to hell, under the load of my sins, to suffer the exact sentence I deserved. I was the one who deserved to go to hell—not him.

As the Scripture says:

> Thou wilt not leave my [Jesus'] soul in **hell**, neither wilt thou suffer thine Holy One to see corruption.[27]

The good news is that having done all this for me and in my place, after three days and three nights in the heart of the earth, Jesus rose from the dead—without the sins he took down to hell **on** him.

After he rose from the dead, he ate and drank with his disciples over a period of 40 days, was seen by over 500 people at once . . .

> For I delivered unto you first of all that which I also received, how that Christ died for our sins according to the scriptures; And that he was buried, and that **he rose again the third day** according to the scriptures: And that he was seen of Cephas, then of the twelve: After that, **he was seen of above five hundred brethren at once.**[28]

. . . then ascended into heaven and someday, hopefully soon, he's coming back again to rule and reign on this earth and fix the mess.

> And when he [Jesus] had spoken these things, while they beheld, he was taken up; and a cloud received

him out of their sight. And while they looked stedfastly toward heaven as he went up, behold, two men stood by them in white apparel; Which also said, Ye men of Galilee, why stand ye gazing up into heaven? this same Jesus, which is taken up from you into heaven, shall so come in like manner as ye have seen him go into heaven.[29]

It was October of 1978 that I realized I was a lost sinner headed for hell. Seeing my need, I received Jesus Christ as my Savior. It was at that moment in time that I was born again.

Like the Scripture says:

But **as many as received him, to them** gave he power to become the sons of God, even to them that believe on his name: **Which were born . . . of God.**[30]

I received everlasting life that very day.

I knew it then, and I know it now. I have everlasting life. I don't **need** to be afraid to die anymore because I don't need to fear judgment. My sins are all paid for by my Savior.

Actually, for to me to live *is* Christ, and to die *is* gain. Plus, the Scripture says:

> There is therefore now **no condemnation** to them which are in Christ Jesus, who walk not after the flesh, but after the Spirit.[31]

I don't fear death anymore because I don't fear judgment and I don't fear hell. The authority for me to believe this is based not on my works but upon the promise of everlasting life offered to me in the Word of God. It is his promise that I believe. And he doesn't lie.

> For God so loved the world, that he gave his only begotten Son, that **whosoever believeth** in him should not perish, but **have everlasting life**.[32]
>
> He that **believeth** on the Son **hath everlasting life**: and he that belie-

veth not the Son shall not see life; but
the wrath of God abideth on him.[33]

That "hath" is in the present tense. God wasn't joking when he made that promise. The verse **means** exactly what it **says**.

Now for the most important thing your religion never told you, but it is revealed in the Bible . . .

7

Eternal Life
Is a **Free Gift**

You can't:

    Earn it.

        Merit it.

            Buy it.

The gift of God is eternal life through Jesus Christ our Lord. – Romans 6:23

It's a free gift. Not the "free" gift that you have to work for like we saw earlier.

> For the wages of sin is death; but **the gift of God is eternal life** through Jesus Christ our Lord.[1]

I'll bet no one ever told you that eternal life was a **gift**. For 28 years no one ever told me. We

125

were always taught that you had to **DO** certain things to get it.

Eternal life is **a free gift** according to the Scripture—**not** something I was required to merit or earn by a combination of faith plus good works, like I was taught. Not only is eternal life a free gift, but . . .

Eternal life is promised to anyone who comes to Jesus Christ.

Think about it, how can any **gift** be **earned**?

If you have to work for it at all, it's no longer a gift. Imagine how insulted you would be if you gave a gift to someone and they turned around and asked you how much they owed you or what they had to **DO** in order to receive it.

That's exactly what happens with God. He offers eternal life as a **free gift** to any sinner who repents and trusts Christ as his or her Savior.

But don't get me wrong, "good works" are commendable, and the Lord is pleased when anybody does them. It's just that they are not conditional to getting eternal life. Clearly, it's a gift. You end up doing "good works" out of a grateful heart—not as a prerequisite to earning what is offered freely.

The take-away to all this is that:

Unlike the Bible . . .

Almost every religion on earth is based on some system of religious works that you must DO to earn eternal life instead of just receiving the gift Christ has already earned for you.

Sadly, all religions teach us to do certain works, perform certain rituals, keep certain laws, pray certain prayers, and do many other things. And even after all this, they still can't tell you when you or I have **DONE** enough to **earn** eternal life and/or make it to heaven.

The Bible refers to all these religious works as "**our righteousness.**"

Yet here's what God says about "**our righteousness**":

> But we are all as an unclean thing, and all **our righteousnesses are as filthy rags**; and we all do fade as a leaf; and our iniquities, like the wind, have taken us away.[2]

"Filthy rags." That's God's opinion of our righteousness.

The apostle Paul said that his people, the Jews, had "a zeal of God." They were performing religious works thinking that would make them "right" with God. And like all "religious" people, they went about to establish "**their own righteousness**."

> For I bear them record that they have a zeal of God, but not according to knowledge.[3]

Unfortunately, they were ignorant of another kind of righteousness—"God's righteousness." Notice the contrasting "righteousnesses" here . . .

> For they being ignorant of **God's righteousness**, and going about to establish **their own righteousness**, have not submitted themselves unto the **righteousness of God**.[4]

It's not that they weren't sincere. They were just sincerely wrong.

All they had to DO was submit to the *"righteousness of God."* How simple, yet most religious people refuse to give up *"their own righteousness."*

The Scripture says we just need to submit to the *righteousness of God.*

The good news is that the righteousness of God is freely given to anyone who comes to the Lord Jesus Christ to receive it. The work to provide it to you has already been DONE by him.

"Submitting" is as easy as "trusting" and not "trying."

He offered one sacrifice, one time, and God accepted it as **enough** to make you **perfect** in His sight and to forgive your sins . . .

> But this man, after he had offered **one** sacrifice for sins for ever, sat down on the right hand of God . . . For by **one** offering **he hath perfected for ever** them that are sanctified . . . And **their sins and iniquities will I remember no more**. Now where remission of these is, **there is no more offering for sin**.[5]

Only one sacrifice was needed. Jesus' sacrifice was enough to make you perfect forever. You can't add to what's already been done for you. If he's already earned it FOR you, then why go around trying to earn it for yourself?

What Christ has already DONE is enough to save you from going to hell, give you eternal life, and banish your fear of death once and for all.

Exchanging my righteousness for Jesus' righteousness was the most lopsided deal I ever made.

The Lord Jesus Christ died for me so that I could live with Him. He took my place as a sinful son of man so that I could be one with him in his place as a sinless son of God. He did not commit the sins that sent him to hell. He took my sins on

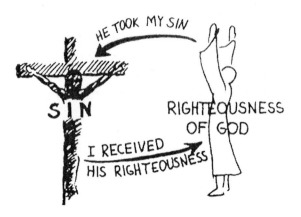

him and went in my place. I did not DO the righteousness that it would take to get me to heaven. He DID it for me. And then he gave it to me.

Two thousand years ago, Jesus "became sin" for me. He suffered and died in my place. He paid the penalty I owed for my sins. He gave his life a ransom for mine. And the very moment I trusted Jesus Christ as my Savior, he gave me his righteousness.

It's no wonder . . .

> **He is able also to save them to the uttermost** that come unto God by him.[6]

The "Jesus" of the Bible is much better than the "Jesus" of Roman Catholicism, Eastern Orthodoxy, Mormonism, Jehovah's Witnessism, and Protestantism, because the "Jesus" Christ of the Bible is able to save to the **uttermost** that come to God by him. This Jesus is more powerful and effective than any of the religions presented in this report—or any other "isms" you've heard of.

The nuns and Jesuits taught me to rely upon my own righteousness (which was based on me keeping the law, and therefore stunk, because I never kept the law).

The Bible taught me to rely completely upon the righteousness of Jesus Christ.

> For **Christ is** the end of the law for
> **righteousness to every one that be-**
> **lieveth.**[7]

I got **right** (**right**eous) with God once and for
all on the day I trusted Christ as my Savior back in
October 1978. That day I was "born again."

I took the Lord up on his generous and lopsided
offer on the day I gave over all my sins to Jesus and
in exchange he gave me his righteousness—freely.

It was the greatest act of love
I ever saw.

I love my Savior who gave his life for me! He
died in my place because he loved me. He died in
your place because he loves you too.

From that day forward, **I knew for sure** that I
had received eternal life. My assurance is not based
on any works I had **DONE** or ever would **DO**. It
is based on what Jesus has already **DONE** for me.

It's not based on keeping the commandments,
attending Mass, or receiving the sacraments. It
was and is based upon the authority of the Word
of God, which not only said I was righteous, but

also said **I could know** that I **have** eternal life right
now . . .

> And this is the record, that God **hath
> given** to us **eternal life**, and **this life is
> in his Son. He that hath the Son hath
> life**; *and* he that hath not the Son of
> God hath not life. These things have I
> written unto you that believe on the
> name of the Son of God; **that ye may
> know that ye have eternal life**.[8]

Go ahead; read it again.

Once I knew I was promised eternal life by
someone who had the power to give it, I didn't
need to be afraid to die anymore.

Wouldn't it have been nice if someone had told
you what God said before now? According to the
Bible, you can know that you have eternal life right
now. Once you have eternal life, you'll never fear
death again.

I know I have it, but what about you? According
to the Bible, the only way you can be acceptable to
the Lord is to trust Christ's work and his righteousness alone and not your own religious "works" or
your own "righteousness."

The Jews once asked Jesus:

> What shall **we do**, that we might work the works of God? Jesus answered and said unto them, this is the work of God, **that ye believe** on him whom he hath sent.[9]

Not hard, is it? The Lord Jesus Christ offers to take all your sins on himself and give you his righteousness instead. If you do that, according to the Bible, God will "justify" you—he will see you and you will be able to say "**Just** as **if I** never sinned."

It's even do-able by a child or someone on their deathbed—like the thief on the cross.

But what about you?

How You Can **Lose** Your **Fear** of **Death** **Right Now**

Most people try to make things "right" with others before they die—especially family. But the most important person you can get right with before you die is the Lord. And yet our own conscience bears witness against us (a thousand times) that we aren't right before a holy God.

My sins haunted me, and yours will, too, until you get right with God through the Lord Jesus Christ. That's the only way you'll have peace and lose your fear of death. If you can find a better way, go for it.

But I can tell you this; The Lord wants you. And the amazing thing is, according to the Scripture . . .

Jesus came to deliver you from your fear of death.

That's right; the Lord Jesus Christ came here to deliver you from the very fear that caused you to read this book in the first place. Look at this verse:

> Forasmuch then as the children are partakers of flesh and blood, he [Jesus] also himself likewise took part of the same; that through death he might destroy him that had the power of death, that is, the devil; **And deliver them who through fear of death were all their lifetime subject to bondage**. He came to free you from the bondage you've been suffering with your whole life.[1]

Want to lose your fear of death? It's easy. Come to Jesus.

If you do, then the Scripture promises that as soon as you die you will be absent from the body and present with the Lord.

> We are confident, I say, and willing
> rather to be absent from the body,
> and to be present with the Lord.[2]

Once you receive the Lord Jesus you will never fear the prospect of death again. Instead of being in the bondage of fear, you'll see death as an opportunity to go to him.

Here's How to Receive Him

God, in His grace and mercy, has made the "**work**" you must **DO** to receive eternal life as easy as this:

> That if thou shalt confess with thy
> mouth the Lord Jesus, [i.e., confess
> him as your Lord and Savior] and
> shalt **believe in thine heart** that God
> hath raised him from the dead, **thou
> shalt be saved**. For with the heart
> man **believeth unto righteousness**;
> and with the mouth confession is
> made unto salvation.[3]

That's the righteousness of God you've been reading about.

The Lord Jesus Christ has already **DONE** all the work necessary for you to receive eternal life right now. Are you ready to receive the Eternal Life he offers?

> This life is in his Son. He that hath the
> Son hath life.[4]

Here are the simple instructions I promised at
the beginning of this report:

Through prayer, ask Jesus to be your Savior.

> But **as many as received him, to
> them** gave he power to become
> the sons of God, even to them that
> **believe** on his name.[5]

This verse doesn't mean you "receive" Christ
in some sort of sacrament like Holy Communion.
It's a transaction similar to what people do on their
wedding day.

They give each other their hearts.

Trusting, not Trying

According to the Scripture, the good news is
that eternal life is received by **trusting** the finished
work of the Lord Jesus Christ who . . .

> is able also to save them to the utter-
> most that come unto God by him,

seeing he ever liveth to make intercession for them.[6]

. . . and not by **trying** to DO it yourself, as recommended by the religions of the world. You need a **relationship** with the Lord Jesus Christ, not a **religion**.

The Lord Jesus Christ is alive, and the great thing is that **he** wants a relationship with **you**.

Getting born again happens once.

Again, it's like getting married. It's a one-time event. You can look back and remember the day. You give your heart to the Lord Jesus Christ and he gives his heart to you. You become one with him and he will never leave you nor forsake you.

You can receive Jesus Christ right now and have absolute assurance of eternal life even if you were to die tonight or three weeks from now or thirty years from now.

Admit to him that you are a helpless sinner and that you'll quit trusting in your own righteousness and religious works.

Repent and be willing to turn away from your sins. The Lord will help you do this.

Believe that the Lord Jesus Christ died to pay the price for **your** sins, was buried, and rose from the dead.

Call out to him now. You can use your own words or pray something like this:

> Lord Jesus, I confess that I have sinned against you in the way I have lived my life. I am truly sorry and I want to turn from my sin and follow you. I believe that you died in my place and that your sacrifice was enough to pay the price for all my sins. I give my life to you right now. Lord, please take control of every area of my life. I receive salvation now, according to your promise, "For whosoever shall call upon the name of the Lord shall be saved."[7]

Thank you, Lord Jesus. Amen.

If you asked the Lord to save you, he promises:

✓   **Assurance**—Him that cometh to me I will in no wise cast out.[8]

✓   **Certainty**—For he hath said, I will never leave thee, nor forsake thee.[9]

✓   **Security**—My Father, which gave them me, is greater than all; and no man is able to pluck them out of my Father's hand. I and my Father are one.[10]

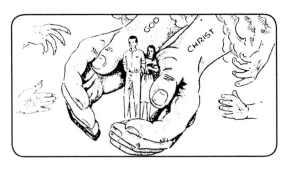

No longer fearing death, and praying the same for you.

– Jack McElroy
Born Again Bible Believer

P.S. If you'd like to know more, visit:

www.HowILostMyFearofDeath.com
www.Hilmfod.com

ENDNOTES

CHAPTER ONE

1. Center for Inquiry, "Love," accessed July 2013, http://livingwithoutreligion.org/love.

2. Jeff Hays, "Facts and Details: Five Pillars of Wisdom, Muslim Duties, Morality and Modernity," accessed July 2013, http://factsanddetails.com/world. php?itemid=1451&catid=55.

3. Wikipedia, "Sacraments of the Catholic Church," last modified August 4, 2013, http://en.wikipedia.org/wiki/Sacraments_of_the_Catholic_Church.

4. *A Catechism of Christian Doctrine: Revised Edition of the Baltimore Catechism*, No. 2. Chicago: Archdiocese of Chicago School Board, 1941, p. 84.

CHAPTER TWO

1. American Humanist Association, "Humanist Manifesto II," accessed July 2013, http://www.americanhumanist.org/Humanism/Humanist_Manifesto_II.

2. Wikipedia, "Humanist Manifesto," last modified June 19, 2013, http://en.wikipedia.org/wiki/Humanist_Manifesto.

3. BBC, "Religions: Shinto," accessed August 2013, http://www.bbc.co.uk/religion/religions/shinto/.

4. Wikipedia, "Catholic Church," last modified July 16, 2013, http://en.wikipedia.org/wiki/Catholic_Church.

5. Religion Wiki, "List of People Who Converted to Catholicism," accessed August 2013, http://religion.wikia.com/wiki/List_of_people_who_converted_to_Catholicism.

6. *Catechism of the Catholic Church*, 2nd ed. *Imprimi Potest* +Joseph Cardinal Ratzinger (Washington, DC: United States Catholic Conference, 1994; digital edition August 2011). (Available: http://www.usccb.org/beliefs-and-teachings/what-we-believe/catechism/catechism-of-the-catholic-church/epub/index.cfm#).

7. Ibid.

8. Ibid.

9. Wikipedia, "Eastern Orthodox Church," last modified July 16, 2013, http://en.wikipedia.org/wiki/Eastern_Orthodox_Church.

10. "Russian Priest Provides Spiritual Care for Hollywood Staff," *Interfax*, February 9, 2010, http://www.interfax-religion.com/?act=news&div=6912.

11.   Adherents.com, "Famous Jehovah's Witnesses," last modified January 16, 2006, http://www.adherents.com/largecom/fam_jw.html.

12.   Jehovah's Witnesses, "Jehovah's Witnesses— Who Are We?" accessed July 2013, http://www.jw.org/en.

13.   Wikipedia, "Jehovah's Witnesses and Salvation," last modified May 1, 2013, http://en.wikipedia.org/wiki/Jehovah%27s_Witnesses_and_salvation, citing: *The Watchtower*, "Keep Your 'Hope of Salvation' Bright!," June 1, 2000, p. 11 par. 6; *The Watchtower*, "Call on Jehovah's Name and Get Away Safe! 'The Way of Salvation,'" March 15, 1989, p. 31; *The Watchtower*, "James Urges Clean and Active Worship," March 1, 1983, p. 13; *Our Kingdom Ministry*, "Meetings to Help Us Make Disciples," January 1979, p. 2.

14.   Ibid., citing: *The Watchtower*, May 15, 2006, pp. 28–29 par. 12; *The Watchtower*, "You Can Live Forever in Paradise on Earth—But How?" February 15, 1983, p. 12.

15.   Let Us Reason Ministries, "The Way of Salvation," accessed July 2013, http://www.letusreason.org/JW37.htm.

16.   *Washington Times*, "The List: Famous Mormons," October 21, 2011, http://www.washingtontimes.com/news/2011/oct/21/list-famous-mormons/.

17.   Giacinto Butindaro, "Salvation Is Obtained by Faith Plus Good Works," The New Way, accessed July 2013, http://www.the-new-way.org/apologetics/conf_salvation_01_obtained_by_faith_plus_good_works.html.

18.   The following points are quoted from Michael Davis, "References: Mormon vs. Biblical Teachings about Salvation," Michael Davis' Mormonism Homepage, accessed July 2013, http://www.leaderu.com/offices/michaeldavis/docs/mormonism/salvation-refs.html.

19.   Ibid.

CHAPTER THREE

1.   Tracey R. Rich, "Judaism 101: What Do Jews Believe?" accessed July 2013, http://www.jewfaq.org/beliefs.htm.

2.   Wikipedia, "Paul Newman," last modified July 13, 2013, http://en.wikipedia.org/wiki/Paul_Newman.

3.   "When Marilyn Monroe Became a Jew," Union for Reform Judaism Online, Spring 2010. (Available: http://reformjudaismmag.org/Articles/index.cfm?id=1561); "Remembering Elizabeth Taylor: The Star Who Chose a Jewish Life," Jspace.com, March 22, 2013. (Available: http://www.jspace.com/news/articles/remembering-elizabeth-taylor-the-star-who-chose-a-jewish-life/13384).

4.   Daniel 12:2

5.   Ecclesiastes 3:17

6.   Luke 10:25–28

7.   Shira Schoenberg, "Jewish Prayers: The Shema," Jewish Virtual Library, http://www.jewishvirtuallibrary.org/jsource/Judaism/shema.html.

8.   Deuteronomy 6:4–5

9.   Faith Explained, "The Seven Principles and Five Pillars of Muslim Religious Beliefs" (blog), accessed July 2013, http://www.faithexplained.com/muslim-religion-beliefs/.

10.   The Qur'an teaches that Allah had no son (4:171, 6:101, 9:30, 10:68, 17:111, 18:4, 19:35, 19:88–92, 23:91, 25:2, 39:4, 72:3, 112:1–3); the Bible teaches that God has a son, Jesus Christ (Matthew 27:54, Mark 1:1, Luke 1:35, John 3:18, Acts 9:20, Romans 1:4, 2 Corinthians 1:19, Galatians 2:20, Ephesians 4:13, Hebrews 4:14, 1 John 5:20, Revelation 2:18).

11.   Qur'an 17:13

12.   World Religions Index, "Table 2 Subject Category: Salvation and the Afterlife," from *The Spirit of Truth and the Spirit of Error 2*. Compiled by Steven Corey © 1986, Moody Bible Institute of Chicago. Moody Press. Accessed July 2013, http://wri.leaderu.com/wri-table2/salvation.html. (emphasis mine)

13.   Shariah Program, "About Us," accessed July 2013, http://www.shariahprogram.ca/about.shtml.

14.   Shariah Program, "Paradise in Islam," accessed July 2013, http://www.shariahprogram.ca/articles/paradise-heaven-life-after-death.shtml.

15.   Qur'an 2:284

16.   Qur'an 34: 3–5

17.   Qur'an 21:47

18.   Wikipedia, "George Harrison," last modified July 8, 2013, https://en.wikipedia.org/wiki/George_Harrison.

19.   Mission to America, "Salvation in Hinduism," accessed July 2013, http://www.evangelical.us/hinduism.html.

20.   Caroline Myss, "World Religions: Sikhism," Myss.com, accessed October 2013, http://www.myss.com/library/religions/sikhism/01_sikhism.asp.

21.   Wikipedia, "Sikhism," last modified August 12, 2013, http://en.wikipedia.org/wiki/Sikhism.

22.   Sukhmandir Khalsa, "What Do Sikhs Believe About the Afterlife?" About.com, accessed August 2013, http://sikhism.about.com/od/sikhism101/qt/Sikh_Afterlife.htm.

23.   RealSikhism.com, "Sikh Beliefs" FAQ, accessed August 2013, http://www.realsikhism.com/index.php?subaction=showfull&id=1248308356&ucat=7.

24. Khalsa, "What Do Sikhs Believe About the Afterlife?"

25. Mission to America, "Salvation in Buddhism," accessed July 2013, http://www.evangelical.us/buddhism.html.

26. *Dhammapada*, chapter 12, verse 165

CHAPTER FOUR

1. Wikipedia, "Thomas Jefferson," last modified June 26, 2013, http://en.wikipedia.org/wiki/Thomas_Jefferson.

2. International Wall of Prayer, Quotes," accessed July 2013, http://www.internationalwallofprayer.org/Q-01-FAMOUS-QUOTES.html.

3. Wikipedia, "Helen Keller," last modified May 31, 2013, http://en.wikipedia.org/wiki/Helen_Keller.

4. International Wall of Prayer

5. Ibid.

6. Wikipedia, "Daniel Webster," last modified June 4, 2013, http://en.wikipedia.org/wiki/Daniel_Webster#Legacy.

7. Wikipedia, "Noah Webster," last modified June 17, 2013, http://en.wikipedia.org/wiki/Noah_Webster.

8. International Wall of Prayer

9.   Internet Movie Database, "Quotes," *Expelled: No Intelligence Allowed* (2008), http://www.imdb.com/title/tt1091617/quotes. (suspension points in original)

10.   Goodreads, "Quotes About Bible," accessed July 2013, http://www.goodreads.com/quotes/tag/bible.

11.   Wikipedia, "Aleister Crowley," last modified June 29, 2013, http://en.wikipedia.org/wiki/Aleister_Crowley.

12.   Andy Greene, "The 10 Wildest Led Zeppelin Legends, Fact-Checked," *Rolling Stone Music*, accessed July 2013, http://www.rollingstone.com/music/lists/the-10-wildest-led-zeppelin-legends-fact-checked-20121121/jimmy-page-once-owned-aleister-crowleys-former-home-19691231.

13.   Goodreads

14.   Wikipedia, "Isaac Asimov," last modified June 29, 2013, http://en.wikipedia.org/wiki/Isaac_Asimov.

15.   Ibid.

16.   Ibid.

17.   Goodreads

18.   Wikipedia, "Mark Twain," last modified June 27, 2013, https://en.wikipedia.org/wiki/Mark_Twain.

19.   Ibid.

20.   Goodreads

21.   Ibid.

Chapter Five

1. 1 Corinthians 15:17–18

2. Qur'an, sura 4 (An-Nisa) ayat 157–158

3. Wikipedia, "Islamic View of Jesus' Death," last modified June 12, 2013, http://en.wikipedia.org/wiki/Islamic_view_of_Jesus%27_death.

4. Matthew 27:63 (All emphasis in Scripture quotations is mine.)

5. Matthew 28:11–15

6. Numbers 23:19; 1 Samuel 15:29; Titus 1:2; Hebrews 6:18

7. Proverbs 23:23

8. Hebrews 9:27

9. Psalm 40:12

10. Psalm 53:1

11. 2 Corinthians 5:10a

12. Matthew 12:40

13. Luke 12:5

14. Matthew 5:29

15. Proverbs 14:12

16. Matthew 7:13–14

CHAPTER SIX

1.   Matthew 22:37–38: The first commandment as given to Moses on the tables of stone in the book of Exodus says: "Thou shalt have no other gods before me." The Lord Jesus Christ cited the corollary, oft-repeated in Scripture, which is that we should love (Jesus') father in heaven supremely. The command to "love the LORD thy God" is stated six times in the book of Deuteronomy.

Different sects have divided the Commandments as given in Exodus in different ways—and this includes Protestants and Catholics. Although the two versions are similar, the differences represent important theological positions. It would be worth your while to compare the two. For now, just know that Catholics omit what Protestants consider to be Commandment 2: "Thou shalt not make unto thee any graven image . . ." (Exodus 20:4).

2.   Luke 10:25–28

3.   Romans 3:10–12

4.   Exodus 20:4–5

5.   1 Samuel 15:23

6.   Exodus 20:6

7.   Psalm 139:20

8.   Nahum 1:2

9.   Psalm 21:8–9

10. Exodus 20:12
11. Romans 6:23
12. 2 Peter 3:9
13. Exodus 20:13
14. Matthew 12:36
15. Exodus 20:14
16. Exodus 20:15
17. Exodus 20:16
18. Exodus 20:17
19. James 2:10
20. Psalm 9:17a
21. Psalm 49:7–8a
22. Matthew 20:28
23. 1 Timothy 1:15
24. Isaiah 53:5–6
25. Hebrews 4:15
26. 2 Corinthians 5:21
27. Acts 2:27
28. 1 Corinthians 15:3–6
29. Acts 1:9–11
30. John 1:12–13
31. Romans 8:1
32. John 3:16
33. John 3:36

CHAPTER SEVEN

1. Romans 6:23
2. Isaiah 64:6
3. Romans 10:2
4. Romans 10:3
5. Hebrews 10:12, 14, 17–18
6. Hebrews 7:25
7. Romans 10:4
8. 1 John 5:11–13
9. John 6:28–29

CHAPTER EIGHT

1. Hebrews 2:14–15
2. 2 Corinthians 5:8
3. Romans 10:9–10
4. 1 John 5:11b–12a
5. John 1:12
6. Hebrews 7:25
7. Romans 10:13
8. John 6:37
9. Hebrews 13:5
10. John 10:30

IMAGE CREDITS

Images not listed come from istockphoto.com

CHAPTER 1

Rausinphoto, Dreamstime.com/; Richard001, via Wikimedia Commons; *A Catechism of Christian Doctrine: Revised Edition of the Baltimore Catechism*, No. 2. Chicago: Archdiocese of Chicago School Board, 1941, p. 84.

CHAPTER 2

Copyright Ryan DeBerardinis; Copyright Feomarty Olga; Randy OHC's photostream on Flickr; Alexander Iosipenko, via Wikimedia Commons; Steelman (staff photographer), via Wikimedia Commons; Diliff, via Wikimedia Commons.

CHAPTER 3

Mbiama, via Wikimedia Commons; Claude Renault, via Wikimedia Commons

CHAPTER 4

Billy Hathorn, via Wikimedia Commons; David Shankbone, via Wikimedia Commons; Phillip Leonian,

CHAPTER 8

Cartoon by E.J. Pace; Illustrations by Mrs. Paul Friederichsen, *God's Truth Made Simple*, pp. 223 and 250. © 1966 Moody Press, Chicago. Used with permission.

ABOUT THE AUTHOR

Formerly an aimless and depressed ex-college house painter, **Jack McElroy** became a serial entrepreneur who found true happiness, success, and fulfillment through a personal relationship with the Lord Jesus Christ (in whose hand *is* the soul of every living thing, and the breath of all mankind), which began when he was born again in October 1978.

Raised as a Roman Catholic, McElroy attended a Catholic grammar school and a Jesuit high school. Once a believer in the Big Bang theory and Evolution, he now passionately extols the veracity of "The Book." He has read through the Bible 18 times (including the 1611 First Edition of the King James Bible three times). He has taught it to all age groups, from preschoolers to adults. He has served as a youth leader for over 20 years and as a deacon at a Baptist church for over 12 years.

Although he attends a Baptist church, he describes his "religion" as a "Born Again Bible Believer."

He has been the president of McElroy Electronics Corporation for over 35 years. He is president of McElroy Publishing and McElroy Rare Bible Page Collections. He was Chief Manager of Minneapolis Cellular Telephone Company LLC and President of Dutchess County Cellular Telephone Corporation.

He holds a B.S. in Industrial Management from Lowell Technological Institute (now UMass Lowell). Jack and Susan have been happily married for 38 years. They have four children and two grandchildren.

Other Books by the Author

Adoniram Judson, Jr. (1788–1850) said, "The motto of every missionary, whether preacher, printer, or schoolmaster, ought to be **'Devoted for life.'**" Now for the first time, you can read and study the arsenal of "soul winning tools" used by "The Father of American Foreign Missions." This is the only book in the world that contains an outstanding collection of the four most prominent tracts Judson used as well as the first translation of Judson's newly discovered fifth tract that he used as a primer on the Old Testament promises of a Savior.

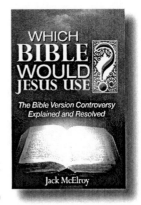

By answering the question "if Jesus came to your church, which Bible would he use?" the Bible version controversy is settled once and for all. This book convincingly explains why the Lord can't use the NIV, ESV, NASB, NLT, NRSV or any modern version including the New King James Version without looking foolish and destroying the brand he's established for the past 400 years. His choice is proven to be the King James Bible.

OTHER BOOKS FROM McELROY PUBLISHING

How to Be a Successful Camp Counselor
by Dr. J. David Burrow

How to Be a Great Camp Counselor
by Dr. J. David Burrow

*The Camp Counselor's Handbook of Over 90 Games
and Activities Just for Rainy Days!*
by Dr. J. David Burrow

*The Complete Encyclopedia of Christian Camp
Directing and Programming*
by Dr. J. David Burrow

*Mastering Leadership in the Christian Camp
and Related Ministries*
by Dr. J. David Burrow

McElroy Publishing
Transforming Hearts and Lives Since 1992

CPSIA information can be obtained at www.ICGtesting.com
Printed in the USA
BVOW01s1029310514

354830BV00001B/1/P

9 780986 026539